# INTO THE BURNING SEA
# THE 1918 MIRLO RESCUE
## AND THE SPIRIT OF DAUNTLESS DEVOTION TO DUTY

*"The spirit of dauntless devotion to duty displayed by you and the members of the [Chicamacomico Life-Saving Station] crew on this occasion is in keeping with the highest tradition of the Coast Guard, and this office desires to express its unqualified commendation of your gallant efforts in the interest of humanity."*

Annual Report of the U.S. Secretary of the Navy
to John Allen Midgett

Kevin P. Duffus photo.

# INTO THE BURNING SEA
# THE 1918 MIRLO RESCUE
## AND THE SPIRIT OF DAUNTLESS DEVOTION TO DUTY

**KEVIN P. DUFFUS**
**LOOKING GLASS PRODUCTIONS, INC.**
**CRUSO, NORTH CAROLINA**

# INTO THE BURNING SEA
# THE 1918 MIRLO RESCUE

©2018 by Kevin P. Duffus

Published by:
Looking Glass Productions, Inc.
Cruso, North Carolina, USA.
www.kevinduffus.com

All Rights Reserved under International and Pan American Copyright Conventions.

Except for the use of brief quotations embodied in critical articles and reviews, no part of this book may be reproduced or transmitted in any form by any means, electronic or mechanical, including photocopying, recording, or scanning, or by any information storage or retrieval system, except as may be expressly permitted by the 1976 Copyright Act or by the publisher. Requests for permission should be made in writing to Looking Glass Productions, Inc., P.O. Box 561, Waynesville, North Carolina, 28786, USA.

To contact the publisher for comments,
customer service and orders, E-mail:
looking_glass@earthlink.net

Book design:
Looking Glass Productions, Inc.

Library of Congress Control Number: 2018906635

ISBN 1-888285-60-4

Printed in China
First Edition First Printing

# CONTENTS

**PREFACE 7**

**DEPARTURES 9**

**CROSSINGS 17**

**ISLAND OF HEROES 23**

**WIMBLE SHOALS 31**

**AFTERMATH 49**

**THE LIFESAVERS' LEGACY 55**

**THE SEVENTH HERO 63**

**NOTES 64**

**BIBLIOGRAPHY 65**

**ACKNOWLEDGEMENTS 66**

*Dedicated to the "Mighty Midgetts of Chicamacomico"
and their families of Hatteras Island and beyond.*

All too often, history is reduced to a simple chronological ordering of events, usually with a strong political or socio-economic focus. Admittedly, such studies are important and frequently provide dynamic insights and perspectives on our shared human past. However, *Into the Burning Sea* is something more than a record of events. Kevin Duffus has a remarkable gift for injecting a genuine humanity into the story he tells.

The crew of *Mirlo*, Keeper John Allen Midgett, the surfmen of Chicamacomico, the respective families, all come into focus and remind the reader these are real people with names and faces, hopes and fears. Consequently, the chronicle of the amazing events of that long-ago day in August become even more engaging and inspirational. It is an extraordinary tale well told.

Joseph Schwarzer
Director, North Carolina Maritime Museum System

# PREFACE

In the spring of 1918, Germany was desperate. The tides of World War I had turned. The Imperial Navy's two-year U-boat domination over its enemies' inbound merchant traffic in the southwest approaches to Great Britain and Ireland had been substantially diminished by the implementation of trans-Atlantic convoys under the protection of dozens of U.S. destroyers and armed escorts. As a result, millions of American soldiers and tens of millions of tons of war matériel, food, and fuel were successfully leaving North American ports and being landed on the coasts of France and Britain, while German citizens were inexorably starving to death by the stranglehold of a four-year-long Allied blockade of its ports. In a last-ditch effort to reverse its fortunes, Germany dispatched six of its long-range cruiser and minelayer U-boats to U.S. and Canadian waters between May and August in an attempt to panic Americans and draw off the U.S. Navy's destroyers from the Eastern Atlantic. The U-boats' missions were to mine harbors, destroy cargos, sever submerged trans-Atlantic cables, "pirate" precious metals, and gather intelligence for future missions. Even though the American homeland's offshore passages and harbor entrances were left virtually unprotected against the incursion of enemy submarines, U.S. naval authorities did not flinch, and Germany's gambit failed. The decision to allow the U-boat "propaganda offensive" along the U.S. coast was not an easy one as it was expected that there would be losses, and so there were. The lives of hundreds of innocent civilians and dozens of ships were risked so that millions of American soldiers, provisions, military equipment, and ammunition would reach the war front in France in the final thrust to defeat Imperial Germany.

# DEPARTURES

### *Tilbury, England, 2 July 1918*

The 425-foot-long steam tanker, looking like a floating Picasso painted in counterintuitive black-and-white cubist camouflage, slipped her massive manilla lines and eased out on the Thames with the ebbing tide. Crowded with a multitude of tugboats, pilot boats, barges, and launches—all dwarfed by dozens of inbound steamships waiting to be unloaded, the tumult of Tilbury docks slowly receded beyond the stern. Twenty miles to the west was the chaos and cacophony of war-time London; an equal distance to the east lay the restless and heavily mined North Sea. In three days, the ship would distance herself from the shores of war-torn Europe and enter the relative peacefulness of the vast North Atlantic. Her destination was the port of New Orleans.

The departure produced both relief and apprehension for the crew of 51 men aboard. Relief, for in the days before putting to sea, the civilian sailors had seen at Tilbury the ceaseless arrivals of hospital transports and the bloody procession of wounded, gassed, and dying from the trenches at the war front across the Channel. Apprehension, because where the sailors were headed there was a chance they might come home in a similar condition—or not come home at all.

They were a crew of strangers, a team of men and boys. Many of the ship's crew of officers, engineers, stokers, greasers, and ordinary seamen had only just met, having been assembled from 30 different ships. Ranging in age from 17 to 58, they hailed from 13 far-flung nations, including Mauritius, New Zealand, Poland, India, and Finland. Most were from the United Kingdom and Ireland. The sole American aboard was First officer Francis J. Campbell of San Francisco. Often in the merchant service so many men unaccustomed to one another produced suspicions and uncertainties as to their fellow sailors' abilities and work ethic, their loyalties, and their trustworthiness. All but two of the men had previously been to sea. Seasoned mariners could usually be counted on to perform their assignments without supervision, but how would they perform in an emergency? Would they crack in a crisis? With luck, there would be no need to find out.

Their new home was the state-of-the-art tanker *Mirlo*, the Spanish word for blackbird. The vessel had been completed the previous year at the prolific shipbuilding town of Sunderland and the Deptford yard of Sir James Laing & Sons Ltd., on the

# DEPARTURES

River Wear along the northeast coast of England. Much of the ship had been built by Sunderland's youth as many of the town's men of age had left to fight the Germans.

*Mirlo*, along with her sister ships *Montana* and *Mendocino*, had been commissioned by the Norwegian shipping company Wilhelm Wilhelmsen, of Tønsberg. The company, however, was not permitted to take possession of its ships due to the war and Britain's ever-growing demand for merchant vessels. Instead, *Mirlo* and her sister ships were requisitioned by the British government on behalf of the crown to serve as auxiliaries for the duration of the war. The Norwegian-owned tankers were then assigned to Liverpool ship brokers H.E. Moss and Company for their operations. Moss oversaw, among many other tasks, the fitting-out and maintenance of the tankers, administration of ships' papers and cargo manifests, fueling and provisioning for voyages, booking of shipments and arrangements for port berthings, and recruiting and hiring of crews.

Captain William R. Williams

The Moss Company chose 54-year-old William Roose Williams to be *Mirlo*'s captain.* Williams, a blue-eyed Welshman from the Anglesey Island shipbuilding town of Beaumaris on the Menai Strait, was born and bred to the sea. Anyone growing up in the latter half of the 19th century on Anglesey, as Williams did, would have been knowledgable and proud of their island's valiant seafaring and life-saving heritage, surrounded as it was by one of the more forbidding coastlines in the world. In 1830, an Anglesey man was awarded a silver Life-Saving medal for rescuing by rope 40 to 50 men, women, and children from a ship that had foundered near Llŷn Peninsula on Wales' rocky coast. But perhaps no shipping disaster had a more formative influence on the tradition of Anglesey life-saving than the deadly wreck of the steamer *Rothsay Castle* in a storm off Beaumaris in 1831. Of the more than *140* souls aboard, just 23 people were saved from the disintegrating steamer by two Anglesey volunteers who imperiled their own lives by rushing to the scene in a small pilot boat. As a result of the tragic loss of life, both a life-saving station and a lighthouse were established at Penmon northeast of Beaumaris at the entrance to the Menai Strait. Over the succeeding years, numerous open-ocean rescues were effected by the

---

*This was a bit of an irony since the English version of the name of the Norwegian owner of *Mirlo* was also William Williams.

# DEPARTURES

island's intrepid lifesavers and their wooden lifeboats launched from Penmon station. For professional mariners like *Mirlo*'s captain William Williams of Anglesey Island, the awareness that there were courageous men on civilized coasts who would dare to risk their own lives to rescue strangers in distress at sea must have been, at the least, a reassuring thought.

In the weeks prior to *Mirlo*'s departure from Tilbury, the ship's officers, engineers, and a few engine room hands worked aboard the vessel to ready her for her trans-Atlantic voyage. Among the men was 24-year-old Third officer Victor Albert Wild. As they were nearing the date of their departure in late-June 1918, Capt. Williams allowed his crew to invite their wives aboard for a tour of the ship and a convivial farewell dinner on the ship's mess deck, where they were joined for drinks by the owner of H.E. Moss and Company, William Molyneux Cohan. Cohan toasted *Mirlo*'s men and wished them godspeed. It was said that the wives were quite charmed by the urbane and humble shipping magnate from Liverpool's Yorkshire House. Annie Wild and the other wives were given a tour of the tanker, where they most appreciated seeing their husbands' sleeping quarters and the commanding view from the bridge.

Third officer Victor Albert Wild

The summer of 1918 was an unsettling time for British merchant mariners and their families. The deadly toll on both sides of the Atlantic inflicted by Germany's new undersea menace, the U-boat and its insidious mines, torpedoes, and artillery shells had been a regular feature on the front pages of London's newspapers—the sinking of RMS *Lusitania* and the loss of 1,198 innocent lives amongst the most appalling headlines. Naturally, for the younger members of *Mirlo*'s crew like 18-year-old Tom Minty, the perils of going to sea in wartime were especially worrisome. Minty, the ship's second Marconi operator, had only recently passed his tests and received his radio license. He had never been to sea and had no idea what would be expected of him nor how he would fare so far from home. His parents, however, were probably relieved that he was not being sent to the Western Front to join the Allied counteroffensive against the Germans on the River Marne where their son might be shot, gassed, or burned.

Minty was described as a nice lad but was looked upon by his older shipmates to be more like a son than a sailor. During the pre-departure social gathering with

# DEPARTURES

the wives, Minty was heard to ask Annie Wild if she thought they would be all right on the voyage to America. "Of course, you will," she replied with a smile and feigned confidence.

The wives of merchant mariners were "very brave women," Victor Wild later observed, adding that they were all well aware of where Allied ships were being sunk by the Germans. Many of the wives convinced themselves that *Mirlo*'s voyage to New Orleans and back to London, a route generally south of the recent U-boat attacks off Canada's Maritime Provinces, would keep them out of harm's way. But not Annie Wild. Later, after kissing their husbands and saying their goodbyes, the wives disembarked from the tanker onto a Thames River tugboat. Annie turned to those standing around her and confessed, "I do not think that the *Mirlo* will be coming back." "Oh, Mrs. Wild, do not say that," one of the other wives replied as *Mirlo* rounded the bend at Coalhouse Fort below Gravesend and disappeared from view.

### Kiel, Germany, 2 July 1918

On the very day that *Mirlo* left Tilbury, the newest of Germany's large but lumbering U-cruisers, U-*140*, commanded by Korvettenkapitän Waldemar Kophamel, maneuvered out of the Unterwarnow Estuary on the Baltic coast and laid a course for the North Atlantic. Kophamel's orders were to intercept and destroy merchant vessels in the busy shipping lanes off New York's Ambrose Channel and in the vicinity of the Nantucket Lightship, but his ambitions would take his U-boat, and the First World War, much farther south.

Nine days later, U-*117*, a 267-foot-long U-boat of the "UE-II minelayer class" and the fourth of six submarines assigned to the American "propaganda offensive," departed Germany's principal navy base at Kiel. After passing out of the Baltic Sea, she followed U-*140*'s course around the Shetland Islands and toward the Western Atlantic. U-*117*'s principal mission was to lay mines at the entrances to strategic harbors and heavily traveled passages off the U.S. and Canadian coasts but when the opportunity presented itself, she was to sink Allied ships with her torpedoes, deck guns, or scuttling charges.[1] Both U-boats, U-*117* and U-*140* would stray beyond their primary operational targets and have a lasting impact on the communities of North Carolina's Outer Banks.

Fifteen days after leaving Kiel, U-*117* spotted and unsuccessfully engaged a British steamer about 450 nautical miles northwest of the Azores. U-*117* also attacked two passing convoys but, due to heavy seas, again failed to produce results. During one attempt to fire a torpedo, the weapon malfunctioned and only slowly "worked its way out" of the tube, revealing a worrisome fault in the U-boat's effectiveness. Five of the nine torpedoes U-*117* launched over the next five weeks malfunctioned.[2] Other mechanical and hydraulic problems further hampered the U-boat's progress across the Atlantic, not the least of which were leaky fuel tanks, a bad evaporator that limited the crew's fresh water supply, and a defective clutch that caused some dives to be aborted. The combination of these problems would have caused most captains to return to port, but none of these handicaps discouraged U-*117*'s young commander, 34-year-old Kapitänleutnant Otto Dröscher, in the least.

The dark-haired 5-foot 4-inch-tall Dröscher was one of the Imperial German Navy's most experienced U-boat captains. In the fall of 1914, Dröscher, in command of U-*20*, became the first submariner to circumnavigate the British Isles, surprising and embarrassing the British Admiralty that had underestimated the range and seakeeping ability of the German Kaiser's experimental new weapon. (Seven months later, it was U-*20*, under command of Kapitänleutnant Walther Schwieger, that sank RMS *Lusitania* off the southern coast of Ireland.) In his next command, the minelayer U-*78*, Dröscher sank 18 ships, damaged two, and took three as prizes off the coasts of Ireland, Scotland, and Norway between mid-July 1916 and January 1, 1918. Dröscher was a determined, daring, and dedicated German naval officer eager to send the Allies' ships to the bottom of the sea. Even though he was likely aware that his U-boat was trailing a conspicuous streak of oil even while submerged, potentially revealing her location to the enemy, Dröscher pressed onward into enemy waters.

Kplt. Otto Dröscher. Courtesy Deutsches U-Boot Museum Cuxhaven, Germany.

The telltale streak of oil, unbeknownst to Dröscher, was not how the Allies were able to track his progress nor the locations of Germany's other operational U-boats like U-*140*. Since 1915 at London, in a rambling warren of rooms, cubbyholes, and closets in the British Admiralty headquarters secretly known as Room 40, the locations and progress of Germany's U-boats were being tracked through the endeavors of hundreds of wireless operators, cryptographers, and intelligence analysts. Wireless receiving facilities in Britain and Ireland, known as "Y stations," had been able to eavesdrop on coded German messages being transmitted between U-boats and their receiving station at Nauen west of Berlin. Each day, hundreds of encrypted messages were forwarded to Room 40 to be converted, when possible, into useful intelligence by using captured German codebooks.

The British Admiralty's wireless service had also been testing the practicality of pinpointing the locations of Germany's U-boats by using new radio direction-finding technology. Each time a U-boat's wireless transmitted a signal while crossing the North Atlantic, radio receivers on the desolate, craggy coast of Ireland were able

"The direct and most ruthless menace of the war—the sea's hidden and undiscoverable grim reaper." *Halifax Herald*. U-*117*, courtesy Deutsches U-Boot Museum Cuxhaven, Germany.

to acquire a compass bearing or "fix" on the U-boat's location.³ The combination of two or more compass bearings from receivers at different locations enabled the Admiralty's intelligence branch to triangulate a U-boat's location within a radius of 50 to 100 miles. More useful, however, they were able to determine the direction the vessel was headed. For example, if a U-boat's compass bearing changed from 330 degrees to 325 degrees after two consecutive radio transmissions, then the Admiralty's submarine plotting chart at Room 40 was updated to show that the U-boat was heading westward, across the ocean and potentially toward North America. Such was the situation on July 19, 1918, when Korvettenkapitän Kophamel's U-*140* transmitted a wireless signal from a position east-southeast of Newfoundland's Cape Race—and his first transmission since rounding the Shetland Islands. The symbol for U-*140* was subsequently moved well to the left on Room 40's huge chart of the North Atlantic. There was no longer any doubt but that the U-boat was headed for the American coast.

Kophamel exercised little discipline with the use of his U-boat's wireless as he frequently transmitted messages back to Germany. As for Dröscher, his radio habits were much more circumspect. No signals were transmitted (or at least detected) from U-*117* until Dröscher's mission was complete and the U-boat was well on its way home. Still, Room 40 was able to track his U-boat's progress based on the various emergency calls coming in from vessels that had been attacked by the U-boat presumed to be U-*117*.

That a few of Germany's U-boats were making their way toward the American coast came as no surprise to U.S. naval authorities, nor was there any doubt what the Imperial Navy's military objectives would be. In the spring of 1917, Rear Admiral William S. Sims had been sent to London where he assumed command of U.S. naval forces in the Eastern Atlantic. Contrary to the optimistic but inaccurate reports published in the British newspapers and the nonchalant attitude of London's theatergoing society about the war, Sims's classified briefings from his British counterparts revealed the enormous challenge the Allies faced in safely delivering American soldiers, munitions, and war matériel to Britain and France against the increasing numbers and successes of German U-boats. "A few days spent in London clearly showed that all this confidence in the defeat of the Germans rested upon a misapprehension," Sims wrote after the war. "The Germans, it now appeared, were not losing the war; they were winning it." The Admiralty shared with Sims intelligence that had not been provided to the press: "These documents disclosed the astounding fact that, unless the appalling destruction of merchant tonnage which was then taking place could be materially checked, the unconditional surrender of the British Empire would inevitably take place within a few months."

Over the next year, the capable Sims marshaled the U.S. Navy's Atlantic Fleet destroyers and convoy escorts to the southwesterly approaches of Ireland and Britain where the natural consolidation of inbound trans-Atlantic traffic became the principal objective of Germany's U-boat war. It was there that the first "Battle of the Atlantic" would be won or lost.

When U-*151*, the first of five U-boats dispatched by Germany for a "propaganda offensive" off the U.S. and Canadian coasts arrived within sight of the barrier islands of the Delmarva Peninsula in May 1918, the mission's objectives were no mystery to Sims, who had already warned Washington of the possibility. Sims wrote: "The Germans doubtless believed that they might create such alarm and arouse such public clamour in the United States that our destroyers and other anti-submarine craft would be kept over here by the Navy Department, in response to the popular agitation to protect our own coast."[4] Sims's assessment was endorsed by his superior officer, Vice-Admiral Henry T. Mayo but caused a significant amount of doubt and apprehension within President Woodrow Wilson's administration. Both Sims and Mayo, nonetheless, were committed to getting American troops, equipment, and supplies through the U-boat gauntlet in the Eastern Atlantic. They knew that there would be losses of lives and matériel in U.S. and Canadian waters due to a lack of defenses; they just hoped that the losses would be tolerable.

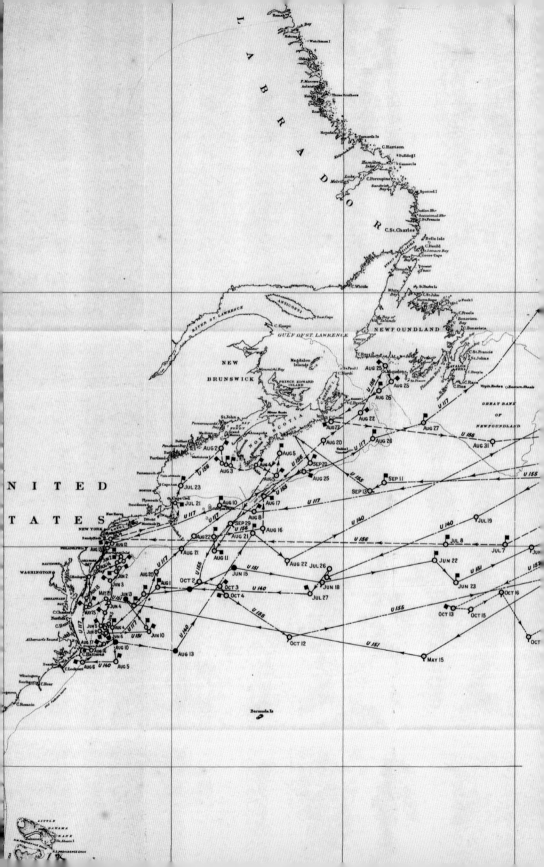

# CROSSINGS

### SS Mirlo, *The Mid-Atlantic, late-July 1918*

Alone on the bridge as *Mirlo* steamed across the empty sea at her maximum speed of 14 knots, Victor Wild took pride in his confidence as the ship's Third officer. Since leaving Tilbury he had adapted quickly to the daily duties, drills, and watch schedules typical of a British merchant tanker. Capt. Williams, too, expressed his approval of his young mate's proficiency.

Wild had previously served in passenger liners where officers and crews were required to dress for daily inspections and for meals in the ships' dining saloons. Without wealthy civilians aboard to impress, merchant captains like Williams permitted their men to dress informally, for which Wild and the other men were grateful, although, the Third officer could have been the best dressed man aboard. Against his wife's advice, he overpacked for the trip, taking with him all of his gear and livery from his liner service. He soon realized how useless it would all be.

Wild found *Mirlo* to be "a happy ship" with all of the crew getting along well together. But the crossing of the ocean was serious business. *Mirlo* voyaged unaccompanied, without the protection of a convoy and armed escorts. It meant that the crew had to be extra vigilant and constantly on the lookout for other ships, especially for the lethal, skulking profile of a German U-boat. Throughout the voyage, Capt. Williams had his crew run various emergency drills for every possible disaster. Even though she was alone on a sea of unforeseen perils, the steamer was not entirely helpless.

All British merchant tankers and freighters at the time were armed with one or two guns and a crew to man them. *Mirlo* had a single, low-angle naval gun on her stern, likely a BL 4 inch Mk VII. Three British naval gunners were assigned to the tanker, a meager contingent to provide round the clock protection. Some civilian vessels went to sea with 20 or more gunners aboard. The presence of *Mirlo*'s three gunners and their gun, however, offered some measure of comfort in the event that they would have to discourage a U-boat attack.

By the mid-summer of 1918, the Allies had gained nearly four years of experience protecting their ships against hundreds of furtive, fiendish, and fatal U-boat attacks. The lessons learned came at a steep price—thousands of lives lost and millions of tons of war matériel and commerce burned and sunk. Germany had been waging unrestricted U-boat warfare against naval and merchant ships exclusively in the seas

# CROSSINGS

*Mirlo* sister ship SS *Mendocino*. Source: *Wilh. Wilhemsen, 1861-1994*, World Ship Society.

surrounding Great Britain since February 1915. Two years later, out of desperation resulting from the Allies' stringent blockade of German ports, the Kaiser expanded his U-boats' anti-commerce operations beyond the war zone surrounding Britain to include military and civilian vessels of both belligerent and neutral nations, including the United States, which finally declared war on Germany and the other member nations of the Central Powers on April 6, 1917.

Upon this accumulated knowledge, *Mirlo* sailed out of the Thames with Britain's most-advanced anti-U-boat defenses available, which, in retrospect, seemed to be rather modest and mostly artistic. The hull of the tanker was painted in a special disruptive camouflage that was intended to confuse the enemy rather than conceal a ship. Termed "dazzle," the idea was first proposed in 1914 to Britain's First Sea Lord Winston Churchill by zoologist John Graham Kerr and was inspired to some degree by nature's way of protecting zebras from predators. The scheme, however, was not adopted by the Admiralty until 1917, when dazzle camouflage was re-proposed with refinements by Norman Wilkinson, a Royal Naval Volunteer Reserve officer and artist who is widely accepted as having invented it. The concept was that a vivid combination of geometric shapes and colors on the hull of a ship would temporarily confuse an enemy observer in estimating the ship's size, speed, and heading. Additionally, merchant ships with two masts like *Mirlo*, would have one mast painted white and the other black, or both in a checkered pattern. Theoretically, a U-boat commander looking through a periscope would have difficulty judging whether his prey was approaching or moving away, causing him to miscalculate a torpedo's targeting settings. The idea turned out to be more effective on paper than in practice. At the end of the war, the benefits of dazzle camouflage were inconclusive, although at least one U-boat commander testified that on one occasion he could not tell if he was observing single or multiple vessels through his periscope. Even though authorities could not agree on the effectiveness of disruptive camouflage, it was tried again in the Second World War with the same disputable results. It is not known what *Mirlo*'s dazzle scheme looked like—every ship's pattern was intended to be unique to further confuse the enemy as to the class of the vessel, whether warship, freighter, or tanker—but photos of other tankers from that time like HMS *Cadillac* in dry dock on the River Tyne offer similar examples (photo on page 8).

# CROSSINGS

Employing another, more-proven defensive measure, *Mirlo* zig-zagged her way across the ocean, altering her heading every 15 minutes while maintaining an overall course to her destination. Zig-zagging made it more difficult for the enemy's U-boat commanders to plan their attack maneuvers and calculate targeting data for their torpedoes.

At night *Mirlo* operated in total blackout, as was required of all Allied merchant vessels, with all portholes fully covered in the officer and crew cabins, wireless office, and mess rooms in both the midships bridge deck and after deck quarters. On some unlucky ships, when exterior hatch doors were periodically opened, the sudden burst of light was known to attract the attention of lookouts atop the conning towers of distant U-boats. "Lights mean death" became a ubiquitous and ominous reminder on posters displayed anywhere merchant sailors gathered during both world wars.

*Mirlo*'s watch standers at night had to be especially vigilant to avoid collisions with other Allied ships as well as the enemy's U-boats. The never-ending tension and exhausting, mind-numbing routine of scanning the horizon for anything out of the ordinary naturally produced occasional false alarms. Anyone who has ever spent a considerable amount of time at sea knows that the infinite combinations of weather, sea, and sky conditions, along with the state of the observer's mental alertness are all capable of playing tricks on the lookouts' imaginations, hence thousands of years of folklore of monsters of the deep. No doubt, many merchant mariners of the time were well-familiar with the nightmares portrayed in Jules Verne's *20,000 Leagues Under the Sea*, of monstrous cephalopods and futuristic submarines. On more than one occasion, *Mirlo*'s watch standers sounded the alarm when they were convinced that they saw the frothy wakes of multiple German torpedoes speeding toward the tanker that turned out to be curious and playful porpoises.

As she steamed her way westward across the expansive Atlantic, *Mirlo* passed only two other vessels. One of them was the enormous HMT *Olympic*, the White Star Line's only surviving transatlantic ocean liner of her class painted in her artistic dazzle pattern of swoops of brown, dark blue, light blue, and white.[5] Since the spring of 1915, *Olympic* had served the Admiralty as a troop ship (hence her designation, "Hired Military Transport" rather than "Royal Mail Ship") and had safely transported more than 200,000 Canadian and America soldiers to Britain, earning the nickname "Old Reliable." Two months before *Mirlo*'s lookouts spotted HMT *Olympic*'s unmistakeable four funnels, the venerable ocean liner, loaded with thousands of U.S. soldiers, chased down and rammed *U-103* that had been lining up to launch its stern torpedoes at the enormous, un-missable target. One of *Olympic*'s three huge propellers ripped open the *U-103*'s pressure hull and the German crew was forced to scuttle and abandon their U-boat. It might be imagined that Capt. Williams and *Mirlo*'s crew gave a rousing hip-hip-hurrah as the stylish "Old Reliable" zig-zagged eastward "at great speed" crowded with Yank infantryman on their way to France to help turn the tide of the war.

# CROSSINGS

### *U-117, Georges Bank off the Massachusetts coast, 10 August 1918*

As the days passed and U-*117* made her way across the ocean, the minds of her commander and crew were occupied with visions of sinking the enemy's great capital ships heavily laden with fuel oil, supplies, guns, ammunition, and thousands of American and Canadian soldiers, and the accolades they would receive upon their return to Deutschland. Instead, at 9 a.m. on the 10th of August, as the ocean bottom rose with the approach of the continental shelf at Georges Bank heralding their arrival on the U.S. East Coast, the only vessels Kplt. Dröscher and his crew encountered were 10 defenseless motor-sailing schooners of the American fishing fleet. The relatively small fishing boats were not the large tonnage ships the Germans were hoping to find, but, as Dröscher may have said to his men, U-*117*, at the least, would be able to supplement her dwindling provisions. Before the day was over, the U-boat plundered and sank nine of the schooners, taking on board practically anything they found useful: food, tools, charts, navigational instruments, ropes and lines, clothes, shoes, and boots.

The fishing boats were helpless. In each assault, the sequence was the same: U-*117* surfaced, fired an artillery round across the bow of its victim, and the schooner made an effort to escape. The U-boat then fired a second warning shot, and the schooner's crew lowered their sails, launched their dories, and rowed away. Dröscher, or his first officer, then beckoned the schooner's crew to come alongside the U-boat to communicate. Next, a boarding party was sent over to the schooner to pilfer stores (Snider's Catsup was among the more treasured of the submariners' acquisitions) and gather intelligence materials in the form of ship's papers, daily logbooks, sailing instructions, newspapers, and magazines. After pillaging their prey, the Germans hung small timed explosive devices to the sides of the fishing vessels to sink them. About seven to 10 minutes later, as the scuttling crew of their first victim rowed away, the schooner blew up with a muffled explosion. In one instance, an officer of the U-boat who spoke a little English turned to one of the fisherman and said indifferently, "There she is; that is war."

"They looked like a crowd of pirates and were very yellow," said a crewman of the schooner, *Aleda May*, the first victim of U-*117* in August 1918. A small number of the fishermen were invited inside the U-boat, which was described as being stifling hot, humid, and smelling of diesel fumes and other fetid, musty, rancid odors. The interior must have seemed like a claustrophobic H.G. Wells-inspired labyrinth of pipes, valves, dials, levers, gears, vents, fuses, and countless other confusing devices and machines. The Americans who descended into the belly of the steel leviathan were hospitably entertained with pea soup, dense black bread, and rum, most likely in an effort to gather information about the busiest shipping routes, American attitudes regarding the war, and, perhaps most sought-after, the location of defensive minefields outside of U.S. harbors. "They seemed to be very much afraid of mines and wanted to know if there were any that we knew of," said the *Aleda May* sailor.

U-*117* officers upon return from U.S. war patrol.
Courtesy Deutsches U-Boot Museum Cuxhaven, Germany.

(It was ironic for the Germans to fear mine fields since sowing their own mines was their mission's principal objective.)

Kapitänleutnant Otto Dröscher was described by one of his American detainees as fairly short, about 5-feet 4-inches tall, "thick set, round face, black hair, dark eyes, clean shaven, and about 35 years old." Another temporary captive of U-*117* said that "the majority of the crew were dressed in khaki trousers and undershirts, some barefooted, and only one appeared in white uniform." Some of U-*117* crew members had previously been to America, and others admitted that they were tired of fighting the war and that work aboard a submarine was hard. After holding each of the schooner crews for the time that it took for the boarding parties of pirates to do their business and return to the U-boat, the fishermen were typically offered a compass heading to the nearest land, a small quantity of fresh water and provisions (some were even given signed receipts for what the Germans took) and allowed to row toward the mainland. All were rescued by other vessels within a day or two. Throughout U-*117*'s war cruise off the U.S. and Canadian coasts, Dröscher's victims consistently testified that the Germans were at all times courteous, friendly, and concerned for their victims' safety, even though the submariners had destroyed their vessels, taken away their livelihood, and ruined the mariners' morale. Later in U-*117*'s homeward bound journey, when Dröscher was asked by a schooner's skipper why he was sinking fishing boats, he replied, "You are helping to feed America."[6]

From Georges Bank, U-*117* laid a course to the west southwest, passing just south of Nantucket. Fifty-nine miles south of Southampton, Dröscher launched a torpedo at *Sommerstad*, a small Norwegian freighter steaming to New York in ballast. The torpedo struck the vessel amidships, sinking it quickly. The ship's crew escaped the sinking ship into a heavy fog bank and later testified to Naval authorities that the first pass of the torpedo took it just a few feet beneath the keel of the ship but that it made a full circle before finding its target on the second pass. It is not known what caused the torpedo to behave erratically—if, in fact, Capt. George Hansen's crew had not imagined it (acoustic and magnetic guided torpedoes and pre-programmed pattern running torpedoes would not be invented until the 1940s). As it happened, it was lucky that U-*117* was not sunk by her own torpedo. The result, regardless, was that Dröscher and his men were no longer just pirating fishing boats but beginning to tally their hoped-for tonnage even if the freighter was not carrying cargo.

U-*117* next ran toward Barnegat Inlet to commence her primary mission of laying mines, but before she could get started, she encountered the Boston-bound 7,127-ton American tanker *Frederick R. Kellogg* loaded with 7,600 barrels of crude oil just five miles off the New Jersey beach. The ship was struck in the engine room by a torpedo, killing three crewmen, and sank stern first in shallow water in just 15 seconds while the forward third of the ship remained above water. The tanker was eventually salvaged and resumed service after the war. Dröscher continued underwater to begin laying U-*117*'s first minefield off Barnegat Shoals, abreast of the southern approaches to New York. It would be two months before one of those mines caused the loss of an American vessel—the small, 39-year-old steamer *San Saba*. An unlucky Cuban vessel struck the last of U-*117*'s Barnegat Shoals mines in late-October.

Working her way down the American coast, U-*117* sowed mine fields near the Fenwick Island Lightship and Winter Quarter Shoal Lightship east of Chincoteague Island. The Fenwick mine field, months later, claimed the American cargo vessel *Saetia* and heavily damaged the battleship U.S.S. *Minnesota*. Along the way, Dröscher sank by gunfire the five-masted schooner *Dorothy B. Barrett* and the four-masted schooner *Madrugada*. The waters off the mid-Atlantic states were a shooting gallery for the Germans. There were few coastal patrol boats and even fewer aircraft. None of the Navy's vessels defending the inshore passages and entrances to America's busiest harbors were powerful enough to take on the larger guns of a German U-boat. The toll of ships and tonnage was mounting.

Dröscher had one more minefield to lay—his fourth. He knew that anywhere along the American littoral where shoals and capes caused a narrowing of sea lanes and a consolidation of merchant ships attempting to hug the shoreline made for an ideal strategic location for his offensive mines. At the navigation table in U-*117*'s control room beneath the conning tower, Dröscher tapped his dividers on a chart at a place named Wimble Shoals and its whistle buoy east of a beach called Chicamacomico Banks on the northern end of Hatteras Island. It might be imagined that he informed his quartermaster: That's where I want to lay the remainder of our "eggs." Dröscher was told that they should arrive there around midday on the 16th of August.

# ISLAND OF HEROES

*Chicamacomico Banks and Hatteras Island, Summer 1918*

Throughout its history Hatteras Island has been shaped by nature and by man—by wind, waves, warfare, and by humanitarian works to aid the unknown mariner. Although present-day residents and tourists rarely see the evidence, calamity and death were frequent occurrences. Indeed, shipwrecks have shaped the culture and communities of the island and the lives of its residents for centuries, as much as the wind and tides. In the early 20th century, Hatteras Island might have been called the Isle of Bones, where every mile of beach was once the scene of unimaginable catastrophe marked by the gray, sun-bleached timbers of hundreds of shipwrecks, and where, in the scattered hummocks of sand formed around the remnant stumps of ancient pine and juniper forests, were buried the skeletal remains of countless forgotten seafarers of long ago.

In 1918, Hatteras Island was among the most isolated and least known places in the United States. The seven villages of the 50-mile-long island were tenuously linked by an ever-shifting, often-vanishing sand road—more a myriad of rutted tracks—that wound through woods, across desert-like sand flats, in and around tidal pools and storm breaches. If someone had no choice but to travel between the villages, they went by horseback or horse-drawn wagons and carts, or walked. Automobiles on Hatteras Island were non-existent. There were no bridges or ferries. There were no telephones except between Coast Guard stations. News, information, and gossip was passed from door-to-door or at church on Sunday. Indeed, it was an age when the only news that mattered—news that had a direct impact on their lives—was what was happening in their own villages. For most residents of the historic settlements of Chicamacomico (Rodanthe, Waves, and Salvo), Kinnakeet (Avon), The Cape (Buxton), Trent (Frisco), and Hatteras, communication with the mainland was limited to mail carried by grocery boats, or word of mouth fishing vessels, or sailing skiffs. By the time news of the world arrived from the mainland, it generally did not matter.

Over time, storms and shipwrecks produced government jobs in the Lighthouse Service, the U.S. Coast Guard, and the salvage industry. On Hatteras Island, the federal government built the tallest brick lighthouse in America—the universal

Gold medal winning Pea Island LSS crew. Author's collection.

symbol of North Carolina's rich maritime heritage—and placed 10 life-saving stations every six miles or so between Oregon Inlet and Hatteras Inlet. No matter how tall or how many lighthouses and life-saving stations there were, storms regularly drove ships ashore onto the submerged sand bars and onto the beaches of the barrier island. Consequently, the salvage of shipwrecks became a vital part of everyday life on the island. Houses and churches were built and furnished with salvaged timbers and relics of shipwrecks; families were clothed and fed by the bounty from shipwrecks. Much of the livestock—horses, cows, pigs, sheep, and goats—came to Hatteras Island as a consequence of shipwrecks. "It was an integral part of the life for this area, absolutely necessary for survival," said David Stick, historian and author of *Graveyard of the Atlantic—Shipwrecks of the North Carolina Coast*.

Shipwrecks also provided the initial inhabitants. Many enduring island families today trace their lineage to an ancestor who had been washed ashore in a storm and who, weary of the risks of sea-going life, retired and made Hatteras Island their permanent residence. The result was a community woven by a patchwork quilt of humanity tossed from the sea that produced independent, intrepid, resilient, resourceful, neighborly people. And none were more compassionate and valorous than the men who served at the island's life-saving stations.

The courage and steely nerves of generations of Hatteras Island lifesavers were forged by the same unrelenting forces that sank invincible ironclad warships, carved new inlets, and sculpted the geography of the island on which they lived. But as tough as they were, the humble Hatteras lifesavers were ever willing to come to the

Hatterasmen with salvage from barkentine *Priscilla*, August 1899. Author's collection.

aid of those in need, regardless of race or heritage or whether they were friends, neighbors, or complete strangers from the sea.

The names Dailey, Etheridge, Midgett, Meekins, Peel, O'Neal, Fulcher, Jennette, Gray, Miller, Austin, Barnett, and Wescott are indelibly etched into the annals of American life-saving. Time and again, intrepid Hatteras lifesavers left the comfort and safety of their homes and life-saving stations during the most horrifying weather conditions to perform miraculous feats of courage. Often slight in stature but always with enormous hearts and strength of steel, they were fearless, unassuming, and willing at a moment's notice to launch their small exposed surf boats into sea conditions that would strike most seasoned mariners with trepidation and terror. One such memorable Hatteras rescue in 1884 was summarized by a U.S. Life-Saving Service inspector: "These poor, plain men took their lives in their hands and, at most imminent risk, crossed the most tumultuous sea that any boat within the memory of living men has ever attempted on that bleak coast, and all for what? That others might live to see home and friends. Duty, their sense of obligation, and the credit of the Service impelled them to do their mighty best." In our present, media-hyped, "famous for being famous" world, it might surprise some that the lifesavers of yesteryear did not perform their unselfish and death-defying feats of courage for recognition or social media followers; they did those things because it was their job.

In the sultry summer of 1918, the men of the Coast Guard Station Number 179, better known as Chicamacomico Life-Saving Station, were doing just that—their jobs, which day-to-day were typically filled with the more mundane routines of

# ISLAND OF HEROES

taking turns round-the-clock as lookouts atop the watch tower, trudging miles of soft sand on beach patrol, sweeping floors, scraping paint, polishing brass, mucking horse stalls, testing life-saving equipment and communications gear, maintaining the engine in their lifeboat, practicing signaling with blinker lights and semaphore, learning to receive and transcribe Morse code, endlessly repeating life-saving drills with their beach apparatus, and passing regular inspections by the station's keeper. Nearly all of the men of Station 179 were the sons and grandsons of lifesavers, lighthouse keepers, and watermen. Saltwater was in their blood, and their respect for the sea was an intrinsic part of their souls. Day after day they toiled at their repetitive tasks, ever mindful of their life-saving forebears and the island's remarkable tradition of historic, gold and silver medal-winning rescues, never knowing if and when they themselves might be called upon by fate to perform such a heroic feat, or pay the ultimate price for trying. Maybe today, maybe tomorrow, maybe never?

The keeper of Station 179, or commander, was Chief Boatswain John Allen Midgett, Jr., affectionately known to everyone in the Chicamacomico community as Captain Johnny. It should come as no surprise that Midgett's ancestors were lifesavers and his father had once been keeper of the New Inlet Station just a couple of miles north of Rodanthe. Midgett, at the age of 22, followed in his father's footsteps and joined the U.S. Life-Saving Service as a surfman at Little Kinnakeet Station midway down Hatteras Island in 1898.

Midgett's formative first year of training was certainly influenced by an auspicious event just a few miles to the north—Gull Shoal Life-Saving Station surfman Rasmus Midgett's single-handed rescue of 10 survivors of the barkentine *Priscilla* at two in the morning in the waning hours of the infamous 1899 San Ciriaco hurricane. Rasmus's selfless act of heroism instantly became a pillar of Midgett family lore and earned him a rare Gold Life-Saving Medal for "Extreme and Heroic Daring in an Attempt to Save a Life." Rarely and reluctantly did the U.S. Life-Saving Service bestow such medals on its employees. Rarely, because it did so only when surfmen clearly risked their own lives to save those in peril on the sea; reluctantly, because even risking one's life was considered part of the job.

John Allen Midgett

Life-saving was a job, Captain Johnny knew, but honest work well done was one of life's most noble purposes. It was how he was raised, and he knew no other way to live. "He was noted for his honesty, courage and kindness," the beloved North Carolina teacher and writer Nell Wise Wechter wrote of Midgett.[7] "He advised justly, assisted readily, took provocations patiently, defended courageously, and was a friend unchangeably." Captain Johnny was raised to believe that what a person chose to do, and not do, in life often had a profound effect on the lives of others, sometimes extending down through generations, like ripples in a pond to a distant shore. Such was the impact of the choices Captain Johnny made in the summer of 1918.

The days during the first few months of 1918 at Station 179 and the other Coast Guard life-saving stations on Hatteras Island were fairly quiet and uneventful, notwithstanding the ever-present clamor of waves crashing on the beach. Quiet and uneventful, that is, until the summer. Hatterasmen like Captain Johnny could always sense when the weather was about to turn, when Neptune would awaken and unleash his wrath upon anyone who would dare to traverse his waters or live along its shores. Well in advance, life-saving men could feel an approaching storm in their bones and would warn their neighbors to get ready. But in the summer of 1918 there was a tempest of a different sort that was approaching the Outer Banks, a danger that the sentient Hatterasman could not perceive. Instead, off-island newspapers like the *Virginian-Pilot* brought news that suddenly seemed to matter, that the tide of the World War might soon touch the shores of the Outer Banks.

In mid-June 1918, news arrived in the villages of Hatteras Island that a German U-boat had one week earlier captured, pirated, then sank the 3,179-ton Norwegian freighter *Vindeggan* 217 nautical miles due east of Corolla. The submarine that sank *Vindeggan* was U-*151*, built as a U-boat freighter like U-*Deutschland* but converted to a long-range cruiser capable of submarine cable cutting, minelaying, or direct attacks against shipping with torpedoes, gunfire, or scuttling charges. Based on intel from the Admiralty's Room 40, U-*151*'s arrival on the U.S. coast was expected by naval authorities but not the swath of mayhem and devastation she left in her wake. In five weeks, the U-boat sank 20 vessels, damaged four ships (one by mine), severed two trans-Atlantic submarine cables, captured but later released 23 prisoners, and indirectly caused the deaths of 13 people. There may be no better example that German U-boats were allowed to go about their business unhindered by U.S. coastal defenses than the fact that U-*151*, while surfaced for hours in broad daylight east of Corolla, was able to plunder from *Vindeggan* "70 tons of pure 100% electrolyte copper in bars" and transfer it into the copious cargo hold of the U-boat.[8]

U-*151* had also achieved victory in the arena of psychological warfare. U.S. and Canadian media reports of her rampage incited the public's hysteria and widespread frightfulness—"schrecklichkeit," as the term became known—that had been Germany's intended result. Subsequently, widespread rumors and urban legends were spawned that were repeated and embellished 25 years later during World War II that German spies, saboteurs, and sympathizers in America were helping to coordinate

# ISLAND OF HEROES

U-*151*'s activities. Even the ubiquitous and widely believed but false 1940s fable that German U-boat crews came ashore and attended American theaters (in WWI they purportedly attended plays, not movies) was originally conceived and spread in the summer of 1918.

The published exploits of U-*151* put the 10 Hatteras Island Coast Guard stations on a moderate level of watchfulness in the summer of 1918, but it was the news headlines in U.S. papers on the 6th of August that heightened the alarm. Two days earlier, U-*140*, the U-cruiser that had left port in Germany on the same day that the tanker *Mirlo* departed Tilbury, announced its arrival by sinking the 10,289-ton Standard Oil Co. tanker *O.B. Jennings* inbound in ballast from Plymouth, England, during a two-hour running gun battle 93 nautical miles east of the North Carolina-Virginia border. Despite its best efforts to fight back, the tanker took a direct hit in her engine room, which killed two. The other 52 crewmen abandoned ship, and one was taken hostage by the U-boat. The news of the *O.B. Jennings* sinking made headlines in all of the nation's major papers including *The Washington Post*: "Outgunned by U-boat—Tanker Jennings Fought Three Hours Before Surrender—52 of Crew Reach Norfolk."

U-*140*'s historic rampage off the Outer Banks was just getting underway. After stopping and scuttling the four-masted sailing collier *Stanley M. Seaman* 110 miles east of Hatteras Island, the U-boat moved south toward the fertile hunting ground off Cape Hatteras, where north- and south-bound ships following the 10-fathom curve and hugging the shoreline were forced to cut the corner around Diamond Shoals.

At 1:40 p.m. on Tuesday, the 6th of August, and the same day Americans were reading about her in U.S. papers, U-*140* lurked in billows of marine haze when she sighted and fired upon the 3,024-ton American steamer *Merak*. Four miles away, the *Merak*'s crew could only see the muzzle flashes of their attacker through the haze but that was sufficient for her captain to order his helmsman to zig-zag at full speed toward shallow water. The chase was on and after the U-boat had fired 30 rounds at the *Merak*, the steamer ran up onto the shoals and her crew abandoned their vessel. Meanwhile, Diamond Shoal Lightship No. 71 frantically tapped out in Morse code and repeated three times a wireless alarm that was heard by the U-boat: "KMSL S. 0. S. Unknown vessel being shelled off Diamond Shoal Light Vessel No. 71. Latitude 35° 05', longitude 75° 10'."

After scuttling the *Merak*, Korvettenkapitän Kophamel turned his attention to the impertinent lightship which he decided had to be silenced. After six shells from U-*140* splashed in the water around their vessel, the crew of the lightship got the message and hastily launched and boarded their lifeboat. What happened next varies among numerous published accounts. This author had the privilege to speak with Ida Willis O'Neal of Hatteras village, who was 14-years-old in 1918 when her father Charles Willis was a crew member of the lightship. She remembered her father telling her that the Germans gave the crew time to abandon the lightship before they attempted to sink it. "They told him to get off," O'Neal said. "They got in [their]

28

Diamond Shoal Lightship No. 71. NOAA photo.

boat and rowed away, they gave them the time to do it. They didn't kill them. Then they blew the lightship up."

No. 71 First mate Walter Barnett told historian David Stick that they left in such a hurry that his chief engineer left his false teeth behind. Another popular version of the story says that a lightship crew member, Guy Quidley, rowed so hard to get away that he snapped his oar in half. What is certain is that the lightship crew rowed and sailed for nearly six hours before landing on the beach at 9:30 p.m. near the Cape Hatteras Lighthouse. When the lightship crew all walked to their homes that night, none of their families were surprised by their unscheduled shore leave. Everyone at the Cape that day had heard the cracks of the gunfire offshore that seemed to last for hours. They knew that the World War had finally reached Hatteras Island. Within days everyone from one end of the island to the other had heard about the loss of the lightship. At Coast Guard Station Number 179, keeper John Allen Midgett put his crew at their highest level of readiness.

Kevin P. Duffus photo.

# WIMBLE SHOALS

### SS Mirlo, *off Chicamacomico Banks, 16 August 1918*

At the port of New Orleans *Mirlo* took on 9,250 tons of the highly flammable aviation fuel benzol and a lesser quantity of paraffin or kerosene. The benzol, the tanker's crew was told, was going to fuel Allied aircraft that were to bomb the German port of Cuxhaven and likely the nearby Imperial Navy's principal Zeppelin facility at Nordholz Naval Airbase in retribution for numerous devastating German airship raids over London and other British cities.[9] The crew considered theirs to be a noble mission.[10]

For safety reasons, the benzol was loaded in the tanker's 12 forward tanks while the less volatile kerosene filled the two after tanks closest to the ship's boilers and engines. Nevertheless, as she steamed down the Mississippi River, *Mirlo* was a floating bomb. The fact was not lost on the crew of the tanker, who, before embarking from the Crescent City on the 9th of August, must have read with keen interest the AP version of *The Washington Post* story about the three-hour gun battle between the *O.B. Jennings* and a German U-boat in the very waters where *Mirlo* was headed. Before they shoved off, aware of the danger ahead, *Mirlo*'s officers likely read that morning's less-than-encouraging news that included a portentous statement from U.S. Navy Secretary Josephus Daniels regarding the recent attacks and sinking of the lightship off his native state's Cape Hatteras: "Daniels said yesterday he had nothing to add to his former opinion as to the operations of the raiders on this side of the Atlantic—that they are instructed to hinder commerce as much as possible, without exposing themselves to danger. Mr. Daniels said other sinkings probably would follow."

Capt. Williams was given instructions to steam to New York where *Mirlo* was to join a convoy that would cross the Atlantic for the Thames Haven Oil Wharves below Tilbury.[11] Until she reached New York, however, the tanker would be traveling alone and through waters that were known by U.S. naval authorities to have been mined by U-boats. Consequently, after she rounded the Florida Keys and steamed north through the Florida Straits, in accordance with his instructions, Capt. Williams ordered the ship's twin anti-mine paravanes to be deployed.

The most-secret British paravane, or otter gear as it was called in the U.S., was a WWI invention that was said to have saved about $1 billion worth of ships and

Paravanes. Image from USNI *Proceedings*, July 1919.

cargoes during the war, not to mention an unknown numbers of lives.[12] The paravane turned every ship equipped with the mechanism into its own minesweeper. It consisted of a pair of torpedo-shaped devices attached to a vertical wing, or kite, that were connected to the bow of a ship by port and starboard towing cables. When deployed into the water by a small crane, the speed of the ship would force each paravane to span outward to a distance of 100 feet on each side. If the paravane's towing cable encountered the mooring line of an enemy mine, the mine would be yanked outboard of the ship where it would be caught by a cutting device and severed from its mooring anchor. The mine would then float to the surface and be swept away from the ship by the turbulence of its wake where it could then be safely destroyed by gunfire. British authorities considered the paravane to be the most notable anti-mine device invented during the war. The downside to towing paravanes was that it reduced a vessel's speed making it more vulnerable to attack by torpedo.

With her twin paravanes deployed and following the recommended zig-zag tactic of altering course every 15 minutes, the conspicuous black-and-white camouflaged *Mirlo* headed up the mid-Atlantic coast riding the currents of the Gulf Stream. Her three naval gunners maintained a constant watch from their 4-inch gun platform; her engineers and stokers kept up a full head of steam; and her officers exhorted the crew to sustain their highest state of alertness, which was not easy amid the fumes and their fear of their cargo's volatility. Under the unrelenting heat of the August sun, the benzol in the ship's tanks expanded and periodically the valve caps to the tanks had to be opened to release the fuel's vapors and relieve pressure in the tanks. Compounding their incessant anxieties of running into a U-boat or one its mines, the danger of an inadvertent spark igniting the ship's combustible atmosphere kept everyone on edge and wearing rubber boots. *Mirlo*, the "happy ship" during the first half of its voyage, was now dispirited by the crew's nearly unbearable tension.

Third officer Wild had the 9 a.m. to 1 p.m. watch on the morning of August 16th.[13] At that time, the tanker was east of North Carolina's Cape Lookout and Core Banks,

Anti-mine paravane deployment.

steaming east-northeastward at around 8-1/2 knots across the deep blue waters of Raleigh Bay. Wild constantly struggled to remain awake as the fumes from the cargo wafted through the open ports in the wheel house. Periodically, he would splash his face with cold water from a jug he kept with him for that very purpose. Cape Hatteras and Diamond Shoals were ahead but not lightship No. 71, which was by then ignominiously resting 200 feet below on the ocean bottom. At about half past one, with or without the lightship in sight, *Mirlo* would round the eastern end of the shoals and change course to about 20° north and roughly parallel to the 10-fathom curve up to Wimble Shoals buoy. From there, if all went according to plan, they were to lay a direct course to run the 300 mile gauntlet of German mines and torpedoes to the approaches of New York.

At 1 p.m., Second officer James Burns came up to the bridge to relieve Wild. Wild informed him that they had passed a number of southbound ships during his watch but other than that all was normal. Wild grabbed a bite to eat and came back up to the midships house to catch a nap on a wooden bench wearing only a pair of white pants and a vest. He had a couple of hours before they would pass the Wimble Shoals Buoy at around 4:30 p.m. where they would set a direct course for New York. Exhausted from the intense concentration during his watch and the soporific effects of the fumes, he fell into a deep sleep.

Wild was abruptly awakened by a violent explosion. Loose objects crashed down upon him. The ship shuddered. Steel plates screeched. Steam escaped with a massive exhalation. A great pillar of flame roared skyward. Wild's and his fellow shipmates' worst nightmare had come to life. It had not been unexpected, but the realization struck him like a bolt of lightning—they had been torpedoed! He glanced at his watch—it was half past four. They must have reached Wimble Shoals. Wild gathered his thoughts, jumped up and ran out barefooted onto the bridge deck. A second, enormous explosion came out of the steam and engineering spaces in the aft portion of the tanker. Wild assumed it was a second torpedo.

# WIMBLE SHOALS

The Third officer's training and the captain's regular lifeboat drills instinctively propelled Wild to his lifeboat station on the port side of the bridge deck. The No. 2 boat was gone! Already lowered! How and why? He was in charge of the port boat! Looking over the side he could see Second officer Burns, who had been on watch on the bridge at the moment of the first explosion. Burns must have panicked and forgotten his emergency lifeboat assignment. Worse—he should have waited to take more men. Wild could then see another problem—as it was lowering, the 25-foot-long port lifeboat with Burns and 14 other men in it got caught in the paravane control lines that were used to bring the device back aboard. The lifeboat tripped on the lines and capsized, and all the men in it were tossed into the ocean. Some were able to grab hold of the upturned lifeboat, while others could not.

The flames were spreading. Masses of burning paraffin were erupting up out of the tanks and then back down into the funnel. Wild ran back to the deck house and into the starboard side wireless room. The ship's senior Marconi operator, 24-year-old Albert Beckham, was on his hands and knees beneath the console trying to wire-up the emergency hand-powered wireless transmitter. "What are you doing?" Wild shouted. "Get the hell out of here! The entire aft portion of *Mirlo* is on fire."

Wild went back into the wheelhouse where he found Capt. Williams who had been trying to assess the damage while at the same time steer the ship toward the beach about seven miles to the west, but with her engine destroyed, *Mirlo* was significantly losing headway. Remarkably, it appeared that not a single one of the ship's crew members had been killed by the torpedo strike. The captain had already thrown overboard the weighted canvas satchel that contained the vessel's sensitive documents and routing instructions from the U.S. Navy. Williams determined that the telegraph to the engine room was not working, the electromagnetic dynamos powering the ship's electrical system had been destroyed, and as a result, there was no way to transmit an S.O.S. There was another steamer to the northwest zig-zagging in *Mirlo*'s direction that could potentially come to their aid. Williams pulled the line that set off one long blast of the ship's steam whistle—their only way to call for help. The steamer held her southward course, no doubt not wanting to suffer the same fate.

Williams shouted above the roar of the flames to his Third officer that the starboard lifeboat with 19 men had also been launched, commanded by First officer Campbell. That meant that 17 men were still aboard the ship, mostly the engineers, stokers, and gunners gathered at the stern. There was one more boat remaining—the captain's gig, or the No. 3 boat—yet it was nearly 200 feet away from the bridge still hanging from its davits on the deck behind the aft deck house. Normally the route to the aft deck house from the bridge was via the elevated catwalk above the tanks and down the center of the ship, but the aft half of it was crumpled into a tangle of steel on the main deck by the initial explosion. The only way for Williams, Wild, and Beckham to reach the after boat was by a narrow, foot-wide ledge, or gunwale, running along the ship's bulwark. They had to crawl, "like cats," Wild later said, while the ship lurched on the ocean swells and the fire spread by the strengthening wind, getting ever closer to the tanks containing the highly-explosive benzol. It was only a matter of minutes before the entire ship would explode. "I was not a religious man ... as I was brought up in my early days—then a choirboy— [but] I prayed that we might be saved in rather a hasty fashion."

As they crawled along the port side gunwale, Wild could see some of the men from the overturned No. 2 lifeboat desperately trying to remain afloat in the water, surrounded by flaming waves. One of them was 18-year-old Tom Minty, the second Marconi operator, who, on the night before they departed Tilbury, asked Wild's wife if she thought they would be alright. Now, six weeks later, the awful scene below became forever seared into Wild's memory, for he later recalled that his drowning shipmates in their last seconds of life were not calling for their wives or sweethearts but were calling for their mothers. "What strange things enters one's mind," Wild wrote. "I could see the poor little wireless officer putting his arms up and going down, calling for his mother. "Oh God, I thought, please save me from this fate."

Williams and Wild reached the No. 3 lifeboat and the remaining men worked together to lower the boat. Meanwhile, the buckled deck plates above the engine compartment were nearly glowing red from the heat below as more and more choking black coal ash and white steam belched out of the ship. That must have panicked some of the men because they began jumping overboard. Then, as the captain's lifeboat was lowering and nearing the water, the falls (the ropes and pulleys controlling the descent of the lifeboat) caught fire. Once on the water, Williams and his men had to cut the boat free from the burning falls and get themselves away from the tanker as fast as possible. There were so many men in the little boat that it was nearly impossible for them to deploy the oars and row away. Williams—now captain of a tiny lifeboat instead of a 400-foot-long steamship—shouted for the men to put up the boat's mast and hoist the small sail they called "a leg of mutton." Only then were they able to move away from the tanker as she was in her final, mournful death throes. *Mirlo* was "wailing," as Wild vividly recalled, like a fatally wounded creature. If not bad enough, their ordeal worsened: "One of the [stokers] in the boat went berserk, so we hit him on the head, and he lay quiet," Wild added.

Fire and smoke poured out of fissures in *Mirlo*'s hull and then it happened—the tanks of benzol ignited. "In a few minutes after leaving it, the ship exploded with terrific force fore and aft, at the same time catching fire fore and aft," Capt. Williams later wrote in a report. From above, debris and flames and un-ignited gasoline and kerosene poured down from the sky, further endangering the men in the boats and on the water. "It was with difficulty that we managed to clear the fire and smoke that was floating on the water, caused by the ship bursting and all the cargo coming out." The cataclysmic explosion tore *Mirlo* in half. "Oh, what a sight," Wild remembered. "And then the fire on the water started."

# WIMBLE SHOALS

### *U-117 off Chicamacomico Banks, 16 August 1918*

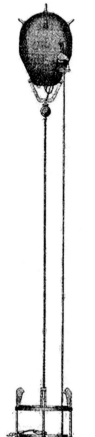

The spectacle of *Mirlo*'s demise had been observed, from land and from sea. At a distance of a little more than four football fields away, U-*117* had launched the torpedo that caused the initial explosion when it struck the ship's starboard side at the No. 2 tank filled with kerosene. Kapitänleutnant Dröscher's U-boat had arrived in the vicinity of the Wimble Shoals whistle buoy two hours earlier after sighting various vessels heading North and South along the heavily traveled sea lane. None of the vessels provided a suitable target. At around 2:30 p.m., U-*117* began the process of discharging and setting her final nine mines—"laying her eggs" in navy parlance—on a line of latitude perpendicular to the paths of the north- and south-bound vessels in about 100 feet of water. Dröscher commenced his mine-laying operations at the eastern end of his intended minefield and then worked toward shore, in the direction of the Wimble Shoals buoy.

The minelaying process was fairly simple. A mine, mounted within steel tracks with rollers and seated on a base that served as a mooring anchor, would be loaded and then launched out of an aft torpedo tube, either while the U-boat was surfaced or submerged. At Wimble Shoals, U-*117* likely laid her mines while submerged because typically German U-boats did not want to be seen, otherwise the location of the minefield could be easily discovered. The mine would then sink to the ocean floor where hydrostatic pressure would actuate a releasing device. Once detached from its anchor base, the mine would be armed and slowly rise on its mooring line to its assigned operational depth—typically around six to 10 feet below the surface. The U.S. Navy reported that German mines usually took between 24 to 48 hours to rise to their operational depth.

While the minelaying operation was underway at the aft end of the U-boat, Dröscher scanned the waters to the West through his periscope in the direction of the Wimble Shoals buoy, sweeping the glass left and right for inbound traffic. His attention was suddenly drawn to port where the white froth of a bow wave revealed a steamship running at full speed about four miles away, coming up from Cape Hatteras. Turning the periscope back to the right he observed another vessel to the Northwest about the same distance away on a reciprocal course steaming a zig-zag course southward that eventually revealed itself to be a neutral Dutch ship. Dröscher decided to suspend his minelaying and attack the northbound steam tanker—SS *Mirlo.*

Before reaching the buoy, the ship abruptly changed course to the northeast—a "zag!" It was propitious timing for Dröscher, as his prey would remain on her new course for a quarter of an hour or so, and now she was headed closer to the U-boat's position. He observed that the approaching vessel was painted in "fantasy markings" and that one mast was painted white while the other was black. This made it difficult, Dröscher noted in his Kriegstagebuch (KTB) or war diary, to determine precisely the ship's heading. He had seen such painting schemes on other ships' hulls but had yet to effectively compensate for the Allies' clever trompe l'oeil. This time he took no chances and maneuvered U-*117* in close to his target as the heavily loaded

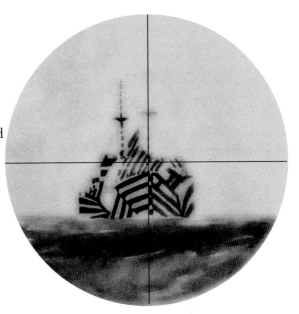

tanker chugged by. The torpedo was set to run at just under 10 feet below the surface. Lookouts aboard the tanker would have had no chance to see it. The target was the engine room just below the stack. "Rohr eins, los! (Tube one, fire!)" Dröscher shouted into the speaking tube leading to the forward torpedo room. In a matter of seconds, the crew of U-*117* could hear the massive explosion through the U-boat's hull. "Vessel burns instantly," Dröscher wrote in his KTB, as his men resumed launching the last of their mines.

### *Chicamacomico Coast Guard Station, 16 August 1918*

At noon on Friday, August 16th, surfman No. 8 of Chicamacomico Guard station, 31-year-old Leroy Midgett, ascended the two flights of steep, narrow ladder steps to the watchtower to relieve his distant cousin, the tall, gangly Clarence Midgett, who had been on duty since 6 a.m. The shorter Midgett settled in for what he hoped would be an uneventful six hour stint in the spartan room atop the 1911 station. There had been a storm somewhere far off in the ocean, and he observed that the cool northeasterly breeze was driving big rollers up onto the beach. Otherwise visibility was good.

Midgett nervously paced back and forth in the small watch room, alternating between the four windows facing seaward as he scanned the horizon through his binoculars. After two hours of mind-numbing watching and pacing, Midgett finally saw a steamship about nine miles offshore, beyond Wimble Shoals whistle buoy, heading south. She was probably on the Norfolk to Florida run, he surmised, not really knowing from where the ship had come nor where it was going, only that it was hopefully on its way in apparent safety. During their careers, the surfmen on lookout at any of Hatteras Island's 10 life-saving stations had seen thousands of ships of countless nations pass their stretch of the beach, and they could identify them with hardly a cursory glance: three-, four-, five-, and even six-masted schooners; brigantines, barkentines, and majestic clipper ships; steam powered tankers, freighters, and the many warships and patrol boats of the U.S. Navy. Every day was a nautical parade off Hatteras Island. It was remarkable, really, all those people out there—who were they, where had they been, and where were they going? Such thoughts occupied the minds of the Coast Guard watchers as they endured their long and lonely duty.

Captain Johnny had put the surfmen of station No. 179 on high alert over the preceding week, ever since they learned of the sinking of the Diamond Shoal lightship. It was hard to imagine that there were German U-boats out there somewhere, lurking beneath the waves, just waiting to sink merchant ships and kill innocent sailors. There might be one out there right now, Midgett might have pondered as his pale blue eyes swept the horizon back and forth. By mid afternoon, things were picking up as traffic offshore increased, dutifully zig-zagging their way north and south. At around three, in the direction of Diamond Shoals, Midgett saw the unmistakeable "white cloud" of a bow wave of a vessel rising up from beyond the horizon—"with a bone in her teeth," the old timers would say. As the minutes passed, the familiar profile of one of the new steam tankers appeared though Midgett's binoculars, with its midships bridge and aft deck house and white smoke billowing out of her stack. She certainly was in a hurry, pushing the bow wave like she was, and rightly so.

No doubt the tanker's captain had heard how dangerous the waters off the Outer Banks had become. The situation must have had merchant captains in a panic. Just a few days earlier, the Chicamacomico crew had to launch their motor surfboat and go out to the South America-bound Japanese collier, *Shakamo*, that anchored close to shore and called for assistance. "What's the problem?" Captain Johnny shouted to the ship's master. "We've heard a German submarine had been seen near Cape Hatteras—is this a safe place to anchor?" the *Shakamo*'s master shouted back. "I wouldn't consider you safe from German U-boats anywhere along this coast," Midgett replied. With that, the Japanese collier hoisted anchor and hurried on her way South.

It must be terribly nerve-wracking for those men aboard the northbound steam tanker, Midgett must have thought. Then, just as the ship was nearing the buoy, she veered off to the Northeast, beginning her 15 minute zig-zag to starboard. What Midgett saw next was almost surreal. Without a sound, "a great mass of water shot up into the air," which then rained down upon the aft portion of the steamer. Then a large cloud of white smoke billowed above the ship's stern. Seconds ticked away and still no sound. It must have seemed, at first, rather peculiar to Midgett—did the ship's boiler just blow? Then 24 seconds later it arrived, a window-rattling, gut-wrenching roar. Flames burst into the sky followed by another ominous rumble. I'll be darned, that tanker was just torpedoed, Midgett murmured to himself. "A ship has been torpedoed!" he shouted to the floor below. He then turned from the windows and leapt through the hatch, practically free-falling down the ladder to find Captain Johnny.

Station keeper and chief bosun mate John Allen Midgett was fully prepared for

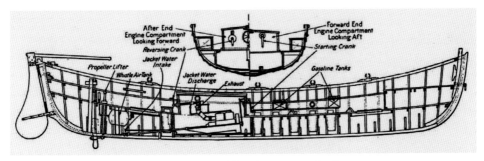

Beebe-McClellan Self-Bailing Motor Surfboat.

the moment. He had rehearsed over and over in his mind how he would respond in the event of a torpedo attack. He, too, heard and felt the earth-shaking rumble of the two explosions. He already knew what happened. He guessed that the vessel must have been a tanker. Lives were in peril. Not a second was to be wasted. Unlike responding to a foundering sailing ship, a tanker on fire offshore called for the quickest response possible. He and his crew had repeatedly practiced the procedure. His men could do their jobs without being told, without even thinking. Captain Johnny immediately summoned all hands and had someone to quickly go recall John Herbert, their cook, and Ignatius Midgett, who had both been out on liberty, they were going to need everyone they could get. John Meekins replaced Leroy Midgett in the watchtower. Another man hand-cranked the station's phone and alerted the other stations. A couple of surfmen rushed over to the stable to harness the horse while others ran to open the doors to the boathouse, which was the original 1874 station. Behind the doors was Self-Bailing Motor Surfboat No. 1046, a copper-fastened, double-ended clinker built hull of cedar planking over white oak frames. Coast Guard regulations required the surfboat to be kept in a constant state of readiness. Already stowed securely aboard was everything they would need for an open ocean rescue including oars, sails, heaving lines, righting lines, cork life jackets for each of the men, eight spare life preservers, signal rockets, a lantern, an electric signal torch, a foghorn, boat hatchets, a medical kit in a tarred canvas bag, and a fire extinguisher.

The 25-foot-long surfboat weighing more than 1,500 pounds was rolled on its carriage carefully down the ramp with a man braking the wheels. The horse arrived and was hitched to the carriage, fresh water and extra gasoline was stowed, and the life-saving crew began the 600-foot-long trot out to the beach. On the way, they might have contemplated, even briefly, what lay in the offing over the next few hours. No doubt their hearts were filled with anticipation, apprehension, and nervousness. Naturally, their first thoughts were of those who were in need of their help. They could see the flames spreading over a large area and the towering columns of black smoke rising high into the sky; they could hear one loud explosion after another over the the noise of crashing waves. What would they encounter when they reached the stricken tanker? Would their efforts be futile? Next the lifesavers might have thought of their own loved ones. It was getting to be late afternoon. How long would they be out there? After dark? Would they come back? Would they ever see their families again? Surfboat rescues in the ocean, especially after dark, were the most dangerous of any method of service performed by the Coast Guard and their predecessors, the U.S. Life-Saving Service. In the 19th century, one Hatteras Island crew went to sea one night on a rescue attempt and never came back.

John Allen Midgett

Zion Midgett

Lee O'Neal

Like marching through a pantheon of marble statues, the legendary achievements, reputations, and integrity of their forefathers towered over the humble lifesavers of Chicamacomico Station as they trudged through the sand and prepared to put to sea, but this was their moment, their call to duty, their chance to make history.

The time had come to put such thoughts out of their heads. Arriving on the beach, they began the arduous process of launching the heavy surfboat. The many U.S. Life-Saving Service and Coast Guard photos of surfboat launchings posed during pleasant weather—when such photography was conducive—utterly fail to convey the lifesavers' often formidable and intimidating task. Facing an angry maelstrom of surf through which they reluctantly had to launch their stalwart little crafts, Coast Guard surfmen had no choice whether or not to attempt a rescue. According to official regulations, "The statement of the keeper that he did not try to use the boat will not be acceptable unless attempts to launch it were actually made and failed..."[14]

On the late Friday afternoon of August 16, the task before station keeper Midgett and his men was daunting, a heavy sea was running. Even though their self-bailing surfboat had a motor, it could not be started and the boat's propeller engaged until they rowed through the breaking waves and made it to deeper water. Because the boat had a motor and was housed in a compartment that took the space previously occupied by a third pair of rowers, launching the heavy boat and rowing it through the bulwark of breaking waves was made evermore challenging.

Captain Johnny assigned five men to join him on the rescue. Surfman No. 1, Zion Midgett manned the oar on the starboard after thwart immediately in front of the engine compartment, while Lee O'Neal, surfman No. 5 manned the oar to his left. Forward of Midgett and O'Neal sat surfman No. 8 Leroy Midgett to port and surfman No. 6 Clarence Midgett to starboard. While they were rowing, the oarsmen faced aft and they could not see the huge waves about to engulf their boat. Positioned behind the engine compartment and in charge of its operation was Arthur Midgett, the son of gold lifesaving medal winner and legendary Hatteras lifesaver Rasmus Midgett. Behind him was the captain of the boat, John Allen Midgett, who gripped the boat's tiller.

Timing the surfboat's departure required every bit of the captain's and surfmen's skill and experience. The boat was slid off of its carriage and coaxed into the shallow water as waves knocked the men sideways, forcefully undermining their footing in the swirling sand. Holding the boat steady and pointed into the oncoming surf as the men leapt aboard was like trying to control a spirited race horse in its starting gate. Other village men were there to help. At the right instant, Captain Johnny shouted for his oarsmen to board the boat and start rowing for all they were worth, and then he climbed in over the stern. "Stroke, stroke, stroke!" he called, as huge waves lifted the bow of the boat high above its stern. The oarsmen pulled as forcefully as they could, their shoulders and backs straining and their feet braced hard against the footplates in the boat's floor.

Arthur Midgett

Despite their mighty efforts, waves broke over the bow and seawater filled the surfboat faster than its self-bailing system could discharge it making the boat too heavy for its oarsmen to breach the oncoming waves. Their first attempt failed. They returned to the beach to drain the boat. They tried to launch a second time, but again the boat swamped and had to be brought back to the beach. Their third attempt was likewise repulsed by the sea. By now, the strength of the six Coast Guardsmen was on the wane. Launching the boat seemed doubtful. According to government regulations, they dutifully made attempts to launch their boat. There were witnesses who would testify to their efforts. The regulations said that they did not have to try again. An inquiry would certainly absolve them for their inability to perform their service.

Clarence Midgett

Off in the distance the explosions continued, the fires roared, and the smoke blackened the evening sky—men were surely burning to death or drowning. At such times, regulations meant nothing to Hatteras lifesavers. The Chicamacomico crew tried again. This time they powered through the pounding surf and made it into deeper water where Arthur Midgett hand cranked the 12-horsepower three-cylinder gasoline engine, it sputtered to life, and he lowered the twin propeller shafts into position by their hoisting gear. They were on their way.

Leroy Midgett

Meanwhile, spectators from the village of Rodanthe were arriving on the beach, having heard the explosions and seen the ship on fire. The rumor spread that the ship had been torpedoed by a German submarine. The Great War had come to Hatteras

Painting by Austin Dwyer courtesy of Chicamacomico Historical Society.

Island. Diamond Shoal lightship had been sunk the week before, but residents of Buxton could only hear the shots—now, virtually from their door steps, Rodanthe residents could see the war being waged. Among those on the beach were almost certainly members of the surfmen's families—fathers, mothers, wives, sons, and daughters. John Allen Midgett, Sr., may have been among them to proudly watch his son. It is hard for us to imagine what it must have been like for those families, watching their loved ones heading out to the burning sea in a small open boat to go to the aid of strangers while the submarine was still lurking offshore. Perhaps only the families of today's first responders, firefighters, swift water rescuers, law enforcement officers, and members of our Armed Forces can truly understand. The historian David Stick once reminded this author that for the women in the surfmen's lives at such times it was especially difficult: "The wives, the sweethearts, the daughters of those surfmen don't get their names in the history books. They went through as much hell as did the men. It was harder for them, maybe, because they couldn't do anything to help." And so, together the families and neighbors on the beach held hands and watched and hoped and prayed.

As Captain Johnny steered his surfboat toward the burning ship, he noted the time—it was around 5 p.m., within 30 minutes of the first explosion. Their departure was reasonably quick despite the delays getting launched. Slogging into the wind and waves at a speed of three to four knots, however, it was going to take them a long time to reach the scene of the disaster. The lifesavers tried not to imagine what was going to happen to the crew of the ship during that interminable time.

# WIMBLE SHOALS

### *On The Burning Sea, 16 August 1918*

When the benzol caught fire and *Mirlo* exploded, the ship's funnel was thrown high into the air, and the waters all around the two halves of the tanker and far beyond became a vast burning sea, including the tossing waves and blowing spindrift. "One mass of flames," Victor Wild recalled—a hell on water. Wild wondered if his death was near. He began to reflect on his life's shortcomings: "I thought that if I ever was saved I would try and be good, not that I had been a very bad man."

Despite being crowded shoulder-to-shoulder, he and the other men in Capt. Williams's gig tried to paddle frantically as they were being chased by the ever-expanding sea of flames. Even as nearly 300,000 gallons of burning aviation fuel poured out of the two halves of the ship and spread outward, the heat rising into the air drew colder air inward from all points of the compass, making it even harder for the survivors to escape the deadly vortex. "I could feel the heat of the fire and some of us in the small boat began to take off their lifejackets and were about to jump overboard, rather drown than be burnt alive," Wild wrote. And somewhere in the hellish maelstrom were the other two lifeboats.

When the port lifeboat capsized, dumping Second officer Burns and 13 men into the ocean their only chance of survival was to somehow cling to the submerged rail of the boat as it lurched up and down on the swells. Burns, who had already panicked once, thought that it was safer for the men to let go of the boat and swim away, as flames appeared to be only yards away and about to envelop them. Ironically, it was the lifeboat that began drifting away from the hull of the tanker faster than Burns and his followers were able to swim. The men who maintained their grip on the boat could see their shipmates as they went under. Among *Mirlo*'s men who heeded Burns's call to swim away was Tom Minty, calling for his mother to save him. Eight others, including Burns, also drowned. A couple of the men who perished were presumed to have been under the boat when it capsized.

The nature of the fog of war and the reporting of its history is such that unintentional factual errors introduced by the news media and non-fiction writers nonetheless become a permanent part of the historical narrative, potentially misinforming subsequent historians and their readers. For example, Henry J. James, author of the 1940 book, *German Subs in Yankee Waters: First World War*, wrote that *Mirlo*'s starboard side, lifeboat No. 1 containing 19 men was commanded by Boatswain Donalds. The author of this book has traced the source of James's account to a *Virginian-Pilot* article published on August 20, 1918, which quoted a Boatswain Donalds. In a comprehensive 1965 report, National Park Service research historian Edwin C. Bearss identified the ship's First officer Francis Campbell as the man in charge of the starboard lifeboat (no source was cited). Furthermore, a careful review of the ship's roster shows that the only "Donalds" on the crew was 58-year-old William W. Donald, a greaser, or oiler on the

43

engineering staff. The ship's boatswain, or bosun, was 38-year-old Robert S. Willard, a balding man with a bushy mustache from Gravesend on the south side of the Thames across from Tilbury. Because it is unlikely that a low ranking oiler would have been sought for a statement by the Norfolk newspaper over the authority of a senior rating like Willard or an officer like Campbell, it is concluded here that author Henry J. James incorrectly named his source. Consequently, this author attributes the following compelling eyewitness account to either Willard or Campbell:

> The sound of the flames roaring through the hull was like the roar of fire in a furnace under forced draft. The wind which had been picking up all afternoon was reaching gale force. It assisted us down wind away from the burning hulk, but also swept the dense black cloud of smoke which choked us. It also sent long tongues of flame licking the top of the oil slick in which we were drifting. It was dark as night. To windward as far as we could see was a river of flame. I ordered the men to remove their shirts to beat out the flames that were burning patches on the side of the boat. When their shirts were gone, we used our pants. The men were tortured by the flames that seared their oil-soaked bodies. Three were unconscious from pain and exhaustion.[15]

The men in the starboard boat, already on the verge of being swamped, fished three more of their crew members out of the water. "Our danger lay now in keeping our overloaded boat from swamping or capsizing as the seas began to pile up around us," either the bosun or First officer reported. To reduce the risk of taking on more seawater, the less-exhausted and uninjured men risked being attacked by sharks by taking turns jumping overboard and clinging to the boat's lifelines. When the lifeboat drifted into patches of burning gasoline, the men in the water had to dive under the boat to avoid being burned.

Pushed by wind and whirling eddies of the Labrador Current the starboard lifeboat drifted to the Southeast, away from the two halves of the tanker, farther out to sea and away from the Chicamacomico Coast Guard Station. Meanwhile, the capsized port lifeboat with six men clinging to it or on top of it drifted in the other direction, northward past the ship's bow, tossed about on waves of flame.

Capt. Williams, Third officer Wild, and the other 15 men in the captain's gig barely managed to stay beyond the deadly grasp of the burning sea. They were exhausted by their efforts. Some were suffering from shock. Their hair was singed, their clothing smoldering and tattered, their hands blistered from rowing. Williams exhorted his men to stay focused and keep rowing. In the meantime, standing in one end of the gig, he did his best to keep track of the other two lifeboats that had drifted in different directions and vanished into the veritable forest of dense smoke and flames. "We looked for the other two boats, but nothing was seen of them," Williams later testified. "It was then decided to take the boat inshore." The decision, no doubt, was not an easy one for the Welsh captain of Beaumaris, who likely looked toward the beach and wondered what caliber of lifesavers lived along those sandy shores. Little could Williams have

Painting by Austin Dwyer courtesy of Chicamacomico Historical Society.

imagined that they were every bit the equals of the most intrepid Anglesey lifesavers.

"It was now beginning to get dark and my estimation was somewhere in the region of [8] p.m.," Wild recalled. "We had been torpedoed at approximately [4:30] so we had been in the boat for [nearly] four hours—it seemed days.[16] At last I saw approaching us a small boat, and it turned out to be small motor craft."

### Aboard Self-Bailing Motor Surfboat No. 1046, 16 August 1918

At about five miles from the beach, surfboat No. 1046 and its six Chicamacomico lifesavers finally came upon one of the ship's lifeboats, overloaded and barely afloat with its captain and 16 men. Through his speaking trumpet, Capt. Midgett with his Hatteras Island brogue hailed Capt. Williams and inquired if all aboard were okay. Williams in his Welsh accent responded affirmatively but shouted that there were 34 men aboard two other boats that had escaped the ship and one had overturned. He and his men had lost sight of them. Williams said that he feared that all of the crew of the capsized boat had perished but he asked Midgett if he could attempt to search for them. Third officer Wild's memory was that the Coast Guardsman told them that they were at a place called "Rodanthe Island." "We told them that we believed there might be some of our mates out there, but we told him to be careful," Wild wrote. "And this brave man said that he was going to try and see what he could do, but we were not to land on the beach as it was a surf beach but was to just row towards the land and wait for him to come back." The two boats then parted, one toward shore, the other into the burning sea. As they headed toward the beach, Williams and his men glanced over their shoulders as surfboat No. 1046 vanished into the burning mass of wreckage, gasoline, and kerosene.

# WIMBLE SHOALS

When a Hatteras lifesaver tells someone that he would try to see what he can do, they could expect him to do much more than an ordinary man. That is what Captain Johnny did. In his own words, Midgett described what he and his crew faced: "There appeared to be great volumes of flame about 100 yards apart, and the ocean for hundreds of yards covered with flame. In between the two large bodies of flame, at times when the smoke would lift, a boat would be seen bottom up with six men clinging to it and a heavy swell washing over the boat."

The redoubtable Midgett and his surfmen headed in the direction of the capsized boat, entering a blistering and nightmarish maze of toxic fumes, wind-whipped fire, and disorienting, shifting curtains of thick black smoke. Their eyes burned and became bleary from the heat. Barrels of benzol continued to explode, one after the other, the deafening sounds adding to the harrowing experience.[17] At one point, Leroy Midgett, standing in the bow of the surfboat thought that he saw the U-boat rise to the surface not far away. "She came to the surface, her conning tower," Midgett recalled later. "I said to Captain Johnny, there's a submarine right there. They didn't believe me, and I said, 'Well, there she is.'"

Words are insufficient to describe what it must have been like for the men of Chicamacomico Station. They had to seek a way to navigate between undulating patches of burning sea in order to reach the capsized lifeboat. No amount of training could have prepared them for the challenge they faced. The white, wooden hull of surfboat No. 1046 was scorched as it weaved in and out of the flames. "The flames formed an arch right over us," Leroy Midgett said. "We could look through that tunnel of smoke and flame, and then we had to go under it to get that boat." Without hesitation, Captain Johnny bravely steered his formidable little craft through the tunnel and up to the capsized lifeboat beneath the shadow of *Mirlo*'s sinking bow section. There they rescued the six burned but grateful castaways.

The starboard lifeboat overloaded with 19 men was no where to be seen. Midgett's instincts told him that they must have drifted to the south, in the direction of the aft portion of the ship. A trail of debris floating on the surface carried by the southward flowing current pointed the way. If Midgett could not reach them before dark, it was possible, even likely, that the drifting lifeboat with 19 souls aboard would never be seen again.

The Chicamacomico Coast Guardsmen eventually found the starboard lifeboat "drifting helplessly with the wind and sea about nine miles Southeast of the station." First officer Campbell and Bosun Willard were pleasantly surprised to be found by the life-saving crew, but also that there were six survivors from the port lifeboat with them. "We figured there could be no survivors from that flaming ocean and were beginning to question our chances of being rescued when from out of the black wall of smoke and flames we saw the Coast Guard boat which came alongside, fished the men overboard and took us in tow."

Captain Johnny's men tossed a line to *Mirlo*'s starboard lifeboat and proceeded to carefully tow them back toward the beach. It was nothing less than a miracle. Despite numerous perils at every turn including the exploding cargo, the foundering ship, the fire raining from the sky, the toxic air, and jagged debris tossing about in the sea capable of holing and sinking the small boats, any one of which could have produced significant casualties, the Chicamacomico crew saved the lives of 25 men who almost certainly would have perished.

South of their station, the two-boat flotilla rejoined the 17 other *Mirlo* sailors aboard the captain's gig that had anchored offshore, just as Captain Johnny had advised them. In his account for the National Park Service, historian Bearss quoted Capt. Williams, who, in a letter to the owners of *Mirlo*'s cargo, Huasteca Petroleum Company, described the moment when he and his men saw the approaching boats and believed that all of the tanker's men had been saved. "They stood up and gave a great cheer." Sadly, Captain Johnny shouted back that a number of lives had been lost, which depressed Williams's men greatly. Nevertheless, Third officer Wild recalled their amusement that among the six survivors of the upturned port lifeboat was one of the ship's stokers, who was "stark naked" and, at 58-years-old, the oldest man on the *Mirlo* crew—none other than William Donald.

Darkness fell, and the Northeast wind strengthened. After traversing about 20 miles of ocean, Captain Johnny decided that it was not prudent to move the boats any closer to his station, which was two miles to the north. He and his men anchored both the captain's gig and the starboard lifeboat about 600 yards off shore, just outside the outer bar where waves began breaking onto the shore. Midgett told his surfmen to make ready to land on the beach. The engine was shut down, the propellers hoisted, and the boat's oars were deployed. Landing on the beach in darkness and with a heavy sea running was not for the faint of heart. Timing was every bit as critical as it was with the launching of the boat. The direction and speed of the boat had to be maintained perfectly to avoid being breached and rolled over by the waves.

All throughout the late afternoon and evening the spectators on the beach followed Captain Johnny's every move. Other Coast Guard crews from the nearby stations including Gull Shoal Station to the south had also gathered and were present to assist the Chicamacomico crew's return to the beach. Bright, battery-powered lights were turned on to guide the island's heroes ashore. The first landing with the survivors of *Mirlo*'s capsized port lifeboat was executed flawlessly. Immediately, the six nearly naked and burned merchant sailors were put on a horse-drawn wagon and transported up the beach to the Chicamacomico station.

Despite their long, exhausting ordeal, Captain Johnny and his five surfmen had more work to do. As tired as they must have been, they launched surfboat No. 1046 four more times through a pass in the breakers to collect the other 36 survivors of the *Mirlo* disaster. Four more times they had to row their heavy boat into the powerful force of the incoming surf; four more times they had to skillfully maneuver their surfboat back to the beach in darkness. For the men of the stricken tanker crowded in the Coast Guard surfboat, the ride ashore was both terrifying and exhilarating. "It was the first time that I had been on the top of a wave and carried right onto the beach," Wild remembered. He and Capt. Williams were among the last of the men to be brought ashore. The time was 9 p.m.

Horses and wagons shuttled the injured and weaker members of *Mirlo*'s crew while others trudged through the sand and broken shells toward the village of Rodanthe. Capt. Williams and Third officer Wild—perhaps in addition to other officers unnamed in the accounts—were later taken to the home of John Allen Midgett. "At last we were all ashore, but we had to walk some distance to the house of the Midgetts family, and as I was without boots, it was a bit hard going on the pebble beach, but it was grand to be alive."

At Chicamacomico Coast Guard Station there was a beehive of activity as dozens of survivors were brought in and offered first aid for their burns, broken bones, sprains, and cuts. The men were also provided dry clothing, food, hot coffee, and fresh water, assisted by the lifesavers' families and the villagers. "That was some time," John Herbert, the station's cook, said in an interview 59 years later. "We fed 60 people that night. Captain Johnny and the surfmen did a job. I even had to take the watch that night. You can take a man to sea in a calm, but when she boils, that's a different story."[18] "The kindness and consideration of the lifesavers undoubtedly saved our men from suffering from shock," Capt. Williams said. Captain John Allen Midgett and his men had performed "one of the bravest deeds which I have ever seen by entering into the fires as they apparently did." That was a supreme compliment from a man who hailed from an island where its stouthearted lifesavers were noted for extreme bravery, dedication, and endurance. The Welsh mariner was clearly awed by the character of the Hatteras Island lifesavers.

Back down the beach, Captain Johnny and his crew, assisted by the men of Gull Shoal Station, brought in *Mirlo*'s lifeboats along with their own station's boat and secured all three for the night in the sand above the high tide line. By the time Midgett and his crew got back to their station and he signed his log for the day's activities, the time was 11 p.m. Another chapter in the storied history of Hatteras Island life-saving was in the books. When Capt. Williams finally got a good look at them under the oil lights of the Coast Guard Station, he observed that "the eyes of all of the life-saving crew were all bloodshot, which was caused by their getting so close to the fire as to be partly gassed and smoke into their eyes."

At the Midgett home, John Allen's wife Jazania hosted *Mirlo*'s officers and served them steaming bowls of delicious soup. The men were told that they would be the Midgett's guests until transportation could be arranged to take them on to New York. "We were treated wonderfully," Victor Wild remembered. "There was a child about 10-years-old [John Allen's daughter, Bethany] who said I could have her room which overlooked the beach."

What a bewildering experience it must have been for Wild, who less than 12 hours earlier had been asleep on the wooden bench aft of the bridge as *Mirlo* steamed north through the Graveyard of the Atlantic and who was now attempting to fall asleep in a young girl's bed on the sandy island overlooking the same ocean waters. Wild's mind flashed through all that had happened. Sleep would not come easily, as exhausted as he was. His thoughts turned to his fellow crew members—of young Tom Minty, Jim Burns, and the others—and the bitter fortunes of war. "As I lay in that bed, it seemed as if the whole of the world was alight. I thought of my dear mates somewhere out there and I had a notion that some of them were still out there, and alive."

# AFTERMATH

## *Chicamacomico Coast Guard Station, 17 August 1918*

**W**hile the lifesavers and the *Mirlo* survivors were sleeping, a flurry of activity was occurring at Coast Guard and Navy offices on the mainland.

Not long after Captain Johnny sounded the alarm at 4:30 p.m. Friday afternoon, the Coast Guard District Superintendent at Elizabeth City, Third Lieutenant Edgar Chadwick, was notified of the event. He subsequently telegraphed his superior officers at the Fifth District Headquarters at Norfolk and provided them with as many details as were known at the moment, who in turn informed their counterparts with the U.S. Navy. The Navy, losing a public relations battle as well as the fight to defend the American coast, was desperate to gather as much intelligence as possible regarding the *Mirlo* sinking. Coming less than 10 days after the well-publicized sinkings of *O.B. Jennings* and Diamond Shoal Lightship No. 71, it was imperative that the Navy was perceived by the media and the American public to being on top of the U-boat crisis. Chadwick continued to send updates as they became available. In the middle of the night after Chadwick reported that survivors had been brought ashore including the tanker's captain, arrangements were hastily made to send transportation to Hatteras Island to recover the *Mirlo* crew. USS *Legonia II* (SP-399), the flagship of the Commandant of the 5th Naval District, was dispatched to steam to Rodanthe as fast as possible.[19] The sleek 168-foot-long steam yacht appeared off Chicamacomico Banks by mid-morning on Saturday, the 17th of August. Meanwhile, a Navy seaplane was sent down to pick up Capt. Williams in order to get him in front of naval intelligence officers as soon as possible to report the facts of the U-boat attack.

News of *Mirlo*'s sinking was already hitting the nation's newspapers, although due to the government's influence with publishers to minimize the losses to U-boats in the western Atlantic, it was far from a front page headline. Buried on page nine in Sunday's *Boston Globe* beneath a department store's half page ad were two small stories. The dateline for the first story was Beaufort, N.C., August 17, and it reported that the British steamship *Mirlo* had been torpedoed by a German submarine. The second story directly beneath the Beaufort report was one from Washington published on the same day. Its version contradicted the cause of the tanker's sinking:

USS *Legonia*, August 17, 1918.

> WASHINGTON, Aug 17—Reports to the Navy Department today did not make clear the cause of the destruction of the British oil steamer *Mirlo*. According to the Navy's information no submarine was sighted. Naval officers believe she may have struck a mine laid by the submarine, which was operating in that vicinity last week. There is reason to believe that no enemy raider is now in that vicinity.

A century later it is impossible to know for what reasons the U.S. Navy chose to disregard Capt. Williams's testimony that his ship had been torpedoed or why they preferred the notion that the ship had struck a mine. Because there had been initially two consecutive explosions, Williams assumed that *Mirlo* had been struck by two torpedoes, but neither torpedo had been spotted by his lookouts nor the gun crew on the ship's stern. Because the tanker had been towing her anti-mine paravanes, Williams told U.S. naval authorities that "it would have been impossible for these explosions to have been caused by mines—the explosions being 12 to 14 feet below the water line." Despite the fact that Williams was there, the Navy stuck to its guns and disregarded his eyewitness testimony. They were steadfast that *Mirlo* had been sunk by a mine.

In 1920, the Navy Department published a 163-page report titled, *German Submarine Activities on the Atlantic Coast of the United States and Canada*. In a section on the sinking of *Mirlo*, the report stated:

> There were nine other vessels in the vicinity, one within sight of the *Mirlo* and no reports of sighting a submarine were made by any of them. The *Mirlo* was located at the time of her destruction over a now well-known mine field. (See Chart No. 2.) The USS *Taylor* sighted a floating mine the next day one mile East of the wreck. It, therefore, seems highly probable that the *Mirlo* was sunk by a submerged anchored mine, notwithstanding the captain's very positive statement that the ship was torpedoed.

J.A. Midgett, Jr. and surfboat No. 1046 deliver *Mirlo* survivors to USS *Legonia*, off Rodanthe, August 17, 1918.

The Navy's rebuke of Williams's testimony should not have held water. The vessel "within sight" of *Mirlo* at the time of the attack was the southbound Dutch ship that hastily left the scene despite Williams's call for help with *Mirlo*'s steam whistle. *Mirlo* was between the Dutch vessel and U-*117*, and if the tanker's lookouts did not see the U-boat, it should have been obvious to the Navy that the Dutch vessel would have been even less likely to have seen it.

Soon after Germany surrendered, her U-boat records became accessible to U.S. naval intelligence officials. They would have been able to read Kplt. Dröscher's KTB or war diary. In it he wrote that at 4:30 p.m. (adjusted to local time) on August 16, he temporarily suspended U-*117*'s minelaying operations and fired a single torpedo that struck the loaded tanker steaming northward at Wimble Shoals buoy (he would not have known the vessel's name). A second German document titled "Liste Versenkter Schiffe" or "List of Sunken Ships" attributed to U-*117*, clearly shows that on August 16 the U-boat sunk a tanker by single torpedo.

Furthermore, in his book, *The Victory at Sea*, also published in 1920, Rear Admiral William S. Sims quoted his own cable message that he sent to Navy Secretary Daniels in the spring of 1917 that "Mines do not rise from the bottom to set depth until from 24 to 48 hours after they have been laid." It should have been obvious to the Navy's investigators that *Mirlo* had not been sunk by a mine.

The final nail in the coffin of the mine theory should have been the fact that Dröscher's KTB indicated that he deposited nine mines East of Wimble Shoals. That fact was even published in the Navy's official *German Submarine Activities on the Atlantic Coast*. But the U.S. Navy was so determined that *Mirlo* had been sunk by a mine that it disregarded U-*117*'s own records—just as they ignored Capt. Williams's eyewitness testimony—and claimed in their 1920 report that the U-boat had laid 10 mines, not nine. It was necessary for the Navy to add a 10th mine to the U-boat's inventory because between August 18th and September 5th, the minesweeper USS *Teal* found and destroyed all nine of U-*117*'s mines east of Wimble Shoals. If *Mirlo* had been sunk by a mine, the U-boat would have

SS *Mirlo* crew on stern of USS *Legonia*, August 17, 1918.

had to have laid 10 mines, or so the Navy purported.

Due to the inherent institutional credibility of the government, the fallacious fact that *Mirlo* was lost to a mine became a permanent part of the story in many published accounts, including, Henry James's 1940 *German Subs in Yankee Waters: First World War*, which in turn influenced David Stick's popular 1952 *Graveyard of the Atlantic*.

After a restless night's sleep with men camped in every room and nook and cranny at Coast Guard Station Number 179, *Mirlo*'s crew awakened and was fed a hearty breakfast. By then, the venerable but charred motor surfboat No. 1046—the 7th hero of the *Mirlo* rescue—had been brought back up to the station. At 9:00 a.m., USS *Legonia II* arrived from Norfolk and anchored off the beach. Soon after, Captain Johnny mustered his weary surfmen and prepared to shuttle the tanker's men out to the waiting steam yacht. This time when they launched their boat the sea was much calmer. The Chicamacomico crew likely made as many as four trips through the surf and out to *Legonia* taking 10 men at a time, considering that there were three pairs of Coast Guard oarsmen in the surfboat in addition to Captain Johnny on the tiller.

The Navy had sent down a photographer who snapped a photo as the rescuers and torpedo survivors approached the deck of the steam yacht. Later, after all of *Mirlo*'s men were aboard *Legonia* they were assembled for a group photo beneath an awning on the vessel's fantail. Many of them were wearing clothes donated by the Blue Anchor Society (alternatively known as the Women's National Relief Association) as well as from families of the Chicamacomico crew. Some were still without shoes. The haunted looks in their eyes and the subtle wry smiles on some belied the hellish nightmare they had survived and the sadness they shared for the loss of their nine shipmates. Two of the men on either side of the awning's support post were wearing their officer's hats—the man to the left is believed to be Third officer Victor Wild.

Late Saturday night, *Legonia* steamed up the Elizabeth River and into Smith Creek, where it tied up at the pier at Bute Street in Norfolk. There, standing on the dock to greet his men was Capt. William R. Williams who was reported by the *Virginian-Pilot* to be "spic and span in a new straw hat and new clothes." Seven of his crew were admitted to a nearby hospital for severe burns and broken bones. The newspaper reported that the rest of the crew were less than impressed with how they were being treated at Norfolk: "Despite the fact that they were suffering from burns and had been without sleep for two nights they were taken to a hotel here which did not have any beds for them." They were probably just as happy going to a bar.

Meanwhile, back at Chicamacomico Coast Guard Station, Captain Johnny and his men returned to their routines as lookouts atop the watch tower, sweeping floors, scraping paint, polishing brass, mucking horse stalls, testing life-saving equipment and communications gear, and performing life-saving drills with their beach apparatus.

As for U-*117*, two hours after she torpedoed *Mirlo* and after she deployed her ninth and final mine at Wimble Shoals, Dröscher ordered his planesmen to bring them up to periscope depth. He saw the aft half of the tanker burning and producing heavy smoke (this was roughly the time when surfman Leroy Midgett thought he could see a periscope protruding from the ocean surface). In the distance— Dröscher estimated it was about two miles away— he saw what he thought was a second ship on fire making even more smoke. He failed to realize that he was seeing two halves of the same tanker drifting apart. In his war diary he noted the possibility that a different vessel might have run into one of his mines, which would suggest that he did not know how long it took for his mines to be released by their anchors.

## SS *Mirlo* Deaths

James Burns, (39)
Second officer

Michael Cain, (40)
Fireman and Trimmer

Christopher Embley, (33)
Fireman and Trimmer

Torsten Lagerbalm, (22)
Able Seaman

George W. Miles, (27)
Greaser

Thomas G. Minty, (18)
Second Marconi Operator

Juan Pena, (39)
Donkeyman

Henry Power, (18)
Fireman and Trimmer

J. Williams, (51)
Able Seaman

# AFTERMATH

At 8:30 p.m., as the Chicamacomico lifesavers were preparing to land the *Mirlo* survivors on the beach, U-*117* surfaced and began heading northward. Dröscher again noted that he could see the "two ships" burning in the fading twilight. The two halves of the tanker had not yet sunk and it is still not known when and exactly where they went under for good.

Low on fuel and having mechanical difficulties, U-*117* began her long journey back to Germany, but her reign of impunity did not yet end. Her artillery shells, one remaining torpedo, and the mines she left in her wake sank eight more vessels and heavily damaged three. In three months U-*117* sank or damaged a total of 24 ships. Fifty-four people were killed by the U-boat making her the second most deadly U-boat operating in the western Atlantic in World War I. Dröscher pushed his U-boat to her limits. Off the coast of Denmark, she ran out of fuel and had to be towed the rest of the way to her home port of Kiel.

In an ironic twist of fate, U-*117* was given to the U.S. Navy after the armistice as a trophy of war. The U-boat visited a number of East Coast ports as part of a Victory Bond promotional tour. "Hun Sub Once Threatening U.S. Rests at O Street Wharf," announced one D.C. paper upon the U-boat's visit there in May 1919. Navy Secretary Daniels inspected the U-boat along with his Army counterpart. "U-*117* is now lying at the Washington dock, crowded with men, women, and children, as innocently as a stranded man-eating shark," reported the *Alexandria Gazette*. "This marine monster of its day had caused almost as much apprehension as had the *Merrimac* in 1862."[20] (The German submarine certainly caused more death and destruction than the *Merrimac*.) Eventually the U-boat was docked at the Philadelphia Navy Yard, where it was thoroughly studied by engineers in order to adopt the more advanced German technology for future U.S. Navy submarines.

In the summer of 1921, U-*117* was used as a target for aerial bombardment tests about 60 miles east of the Chesapeake Bay. The U-boat that sank *Mirlo* was itself sunk in about 300 feet of water about 85 miles to the north-northeast of Wimble Shoals, where it remains to this day.

Serving as both a history and a prophecy, Henry James's 1940 book, *German Subs in Yankee waters: First World War*, summarized the results of Germany's U-boat "propaganda offensive" off the American coast in the summer of 1918:

> Six U-boats in the brief space of six months, operating 3,400 miles from their base, sank 91 ships, exclusive of those salvaged, and killed or drowned 368 people. To this total must be added 11 ships and 67 lives lost indirectly through accidents caused by ships colliding at night while running without lights, and being mistaken for the enemy and destroyed by gunfire.

James concluded his book with a prescient chapter titled, "It Can Happen Again." Off the U.S. coast two years later it did, and it was much worse. The lessons learned from U-boats as weapons of war and disrupters of commerce in the western Atlantic in WWI failed to prepare U.S. naval authorities for the next world war.

# THE LIFESAVERS' LEGACY

Even as they returned to their unexciting day-to-day routines at Chicamacomico Coast Guard Station, Captain Johnny and his men were being hailed as American heroes. A few months after the *Mirlo* rescue, all six men received the Navy's Commendation for "Courageous and Heroic Action" from Navy Secretary and North Carolina native Josephus Daniels. In all, 61 American officers and enlisted men received the commendation in the secretary's Annual Report for Fiscal Year 1918. But only the men from Chicamacomico Station were honored with these words: "The spirit of dauntless devotion to duty displayed by you and the members of the boat's crew on this occasion is in keeping with the highest traditions of the Coast Guard and this office desires to express its unqualified commendation of your gallant efforts in the interest of humanity."

Sometime after August 1920, a brown paper-wrapped parcel arrived at the Rodanthe Post Office containing U.S. World War I Victory Medals for each member of the Chicamacomico Station crew, including the six men involved in the *Mirlo* rescue. Contrary to many previously published accounts on the *Mirlo* story, the life-saving crew did not receive Victory medals from Great Britain; instead they were bestowed a much higher honor.

On February 12, 1921, it was announced in London that, upon a recommendation of George V, Great Britain was extending "an extraordinary honor to North Carolina Coast Guardsmen." The Board of Trade voted to award Foreign Service gold life-saving medals for "Gallantry and Humanity in Saving Life at Sea" to John Allen Midgett, Zion Midgett, Prochorous [Lee] O'Neal, Clarence Midgett, and Leroy Midgett.[21] In his recommendation to the Board of Trade, the King said: "The danger from the burning oil, the difficulties arising from the heavy seas, the cool, efficient way in which the operation was carried out rendered services which are most praiseworthy." At the same time, the Board of Trade awarded to keeper Midgett a silver cup produced by the Royal Mint with the following inscription:

(above left to right) Congressional Gold Life-Saving Medal, Grand Cross of the American Cross of Honor, U.S. WWI Victory Medal, U.K. Foreign Service Gold Life-Saving Medal. (right) J.A. Midgett, Jr., holds Board of Trade silver cup.

> Presented by the British Government to John A. Midgett, keeper of Coast Guard Station No. 179, Rodanthe, North Carolina, in acknowledgement of his able leadership in effecting the rescue of the shipwrecked crew of the SS *Mirlo* on the 16th of August 1918.

For reasons that remain unclear, it was not until August 24, 1924, that the U.S. Coast Guard finally got around to awarding the Chicamacomico lifesavers with Congressional Gold Life-Saving medals. As time passed, the enormity of their unparalleled feat of heroism came to be appreciated even more. On the 23rd of July 1930, at Manteo, the Commandant of the U.S. Coast Guard, Rear Adm. Frederick C. Billard, presented Captain Johnny and his Chicamacomico crew Grand Crosses of the American Cross of Honor. By law, the medal could only be presented to those who had already received a Congressional Life-Saving Medal. Only 12 Grand Crosses could be presented in any given year, but only 11 were ever awarded, six of those to the Chicamacomico lifesavers. The citation presented to the them read, "For commanding and manning a boat which saved 42 lives, at great risk to their own, involving unusual and extraordinary Heroism to the maximum degree."

Every few years, an enterprising reporter would venture to Hatteras Island, brave the roadless and desolate land "of sand, sky, water, and wind," and after paying a visit to Chicamacomico Station they would rekindle the *Mirlo* story. Prominent High Point banker and newspaper editor William A. Blair took such a trip with his family in the summer of 1938 and spent some time visiting with Captain Johnny. In an article titled, "Our Eastern Shoals: A Foreign Land," Blair wrote that Midgett often proudly wore his American Cross of Honor but that "one of his most treasured possessions [was] a personal letter of thanks and commendation from the King of England. On such stuff are coast guards made!"[22]

Presentation of Grand Crosses of the American Cross of Honor at Manteo on July 23, 1930.

Nell Wise, a young school teacher from the mainland living on Hatteras Island in the late 1930s, was another admirer of Captain Johnny. It is not known if Wise (who later married Coast Guardsman Bob Wechter) was personally acquainted with the Coast Guard legend, but she knew enough about him to feature him in her book, *The Mighty Midgetts of Chicamacomico*. She described Captain Johnny in his later years as a ruggedly honest, gentle, and kindly man for whom the world held nothing that could make him afraid. He had the gift of making all men his equals [including his friend Franklin D. Roosevelt]. ... For later generations, the example of his life and service to humanity will be an eternal flame ... a flame which will help to restore belief that faith and loyalty to one's fellowmen are still able to lift common men to greatness—a greatness that made America."

More than a great American hero, more than a fearless Coast Guardsman, more than a community leader, more than a trusted neighbor and friend, Midgett was above all a family man and a man of faith. Despite his greatness and well-earned celebrity, he remained humble, God-fearing, and ever mindful of those things that mattered most—his wife Jazania, his children, Nora, Ellery, Bethany, and Herbert, and especially his grandchildren. In late 1937, 61-year-old John Allen Midgett was approaching his 40th year of having served in the Life-Saving Service and the U.S. Coast Guard. He looked forward to retiring the next year. Other able men (and someday women), he knew, would follow in his footsteps. It was finally time to devote his full attention to his family and no longer to the government and helpless mariners at sea. His daughter Nora, on November 11, gave birth to Captain Johnny's first granddaughter, Jazania, named for Midgett's wife. There was much to be thankful for.

Believed to be the last photo taken of John Allen Midgett, Jr., with his grandchildren a few days before Christmas in 1937. Courtesy of the Midgett family.

A few days before Christmas, Midgett signed out on leave from Chicamacomico Station and made the arduous journey across Oregon Inlet and up the paved road to Norfolk on a shopping excursion. On his way home to Hatteras Island, well after dark on a Thursday night the 23rd of December, he motored south on state highway 34 (today's NC 168), his car "laden" with Christmas presents for his family. Fog rolled in from Currituck Sound. It happened so suddenly, in a curve perhaps: a faulty headlight on an oncoming truck, a vehicle swerved, a head-on collision, Christmas presents scattered along the roadside. The gallant hero of Rodanthe was gravely injured. Midgett was first rushed to the hospital at Elizabeth City where he was treated for chest injuries, severe lacerations, and a broken leg. From there he was transported to a larger medical facility in Norfolk. There, over the next few weeks, his condition seemed to improve, but on the 8th of February he unexpectedly declined and died the next day. The news of his tragic death, reported by the Associated Press, appeared in newspapers across the country.

Like ripples in a pond, the significance of John Allen Midgett's life and the choices he made carried on long after he crossed the bar. On the 30th of May 1953, a North Carolina state historical marker was dedicated in front of the Chicamacomico Coast Guard Station alongside the newly paved Nags Head-Hatteras Highway, a noble but abbreviated reminder of what happened there. The two surviving members of Captain Johnny's crew of six, Arthur Midgett and Leroy Midgett, proudly wearing their life-saving medals, were the special guests of honor. Granddaughters of Zion Midgett and Lee O'Neal held Captain Johnny's silver cup while Jazania O'Neal held a photograph of her grandfather. All three women pulled the strings that unveiled the marker. In the background was motor surfboat No. 1046.

Chicamacomico Coast Guard Lifeboat Station no longer served a useful function, as faster rescue craft permitted the consolidation of Hatteras Island's 10 life-saving stations to two larger installations at Oregon Inlet and Hatteras Inlet. In 1954, the station, including its original 1874 building and the eponymous 1911 Chicama-

(left) 1953 dedication of *Mirlo* Rescue historic marker. (right) Jazania Midgett christens USCGC *Midgett* with J.A. Midgett, Jr., great-graddaughter Jonna Midgett in 2017. Photo by Andrew Young, Courtesy Ingalls Shipbuilding.

comico-type building designed by Life-Saving Service architect Victor Mendleheff, was decommissioned and temporarily transferred to the care of the National Park Service. Gradually over the years, lack of maintenance and the unrelenting winds and rains took a toll on the abandoned structures and the hallowed grounds of Coast Guard history. The future of the station was in jeopardy; its buildings could have become private cottages or a restaurant like the former Kitty Hawk Life-Saving Station, or they might have been razed for the construction of a new housing development or oceanfront condominiums. No doubt, had it not been for Captain Johnny's decision in August 1918 to attempt to launch his surfboat for a fourth time and brave the burning sea to rescue *Mirlo*'s men, Chicamacomico Station could have been lost forever. The station's national historical significance and the heroic efforts of its men demanded that it be preserved. Since 1974, when the Chicamacomico Historical Association was formed through the leadership of advocates Woodrow Edwards, David Stick, artist Carolista Baum, and their many dedicated successors, the station has developed into what has been touted as the "best-preserved and most-authentic of all life-saving stations."

In March 1972, recognizing John Allen Midgett's contribution to the valorous reputation of the U.S. Coast Guard and in honor of the "Mighty Midgetts" of Chicamacomico Banks, a high-endurance cutter was commissioned and named, USCGC *Midgett* (WHEC-726). At her christening ceremony at Morehead City, North Carolina, featured in an issue of National Geographic, Coast Guard Academy graduate Lt. Commander John C. Midgett Jr. proudly stood before more than a hundred Midgett family members gathered on the cutter's foredeck and bridge wings. Forty-five years later, the cutter *Midgett* was replaced with a state-of-the-art, Legend-class National Security cutter, WMSL 757, that proudly carries on the Midgett name and the family's dedication to duty. On December 9, 2017, at Pascagoula, Mississippi, the sleek 418-foot-long cutter, considered to be one of the Coast Guard's flagships, was christened by Captain Johnny's granddaughter Jazania O'Neal watched by 60 Midgett family members. The ripples in the pond—the lifesaver's legacy—reached further than anyone could have imagined in 1918.

The story of the remarkable *Mirlo* rescue has been retold many times over the years in newspapers, magazines, and in books. The narrative primarily based on the official reports of Captain William R. Williams and Captain John Allen Midgett has changed little over time. But there was one perspective of the historic event that until now has not been told: *Mirlo* Third officer Wild's story.

### *London, England, 1970*

Victor Albert Wild could never forget what he experienced at Wimble Shoals off Rodanthe in 1918. The visions of his drowning shipmates, the seemingly inescapable fires, the heroic efforts of the dauntless men in the little motor surfboat, the pretty young daughter of Capt. Midgett who loaned him her bedroom, each moment filled his mind and reoccurred in his dreams for the rest of his life.

Wild's wife Annie was six months pregnant when he departed Tilbury aboard *Mirlo* in July 1918. When news of the tanker's destruction by a German U-boat reached England, Annie was mistakingly informed that her husband had been killed, along with Capt. Williams. The chaos of the final months of the Great War and the deficiency of communications in 1918 left Annie thinking she was a widow. What a surprise and a relief it must have been when *Mirlo*'s third mate returned home safe and sound. A month later, on the 10th of October, their daughter was born. They named her Joan Mirlo Wild.

Wild remained in the merchant service and served under Capt. Williams on two other vessels. He later entered the Royal Navy Volunteer Reserve and served as a lieutenant at the shore-based basic training installation known as HMS *Raleigh* in Cornwall. As the years passed, the hustle and bustle of life gradually pushed the tumult of 1918 and the *Mirlo* story to the back of Wild's mind. But every time he looked at his family he never failed to remember those six brave men in the little motor surfboat.

In 1970 Wild was nearing his 76th birthday, his memory gradually fading. He was curious if any of the valiant lifesavers from Rodanthe were still alive. His daughter Mirlo encouraged him to find out. Without the names and addresses of the men, Wild wrote a letter.

> Dear Sir or Madam:
> An oil tanker by the name of *Mirlo* was torpedoed in 191[8] off Rodanthe Island, Cape Hatteras & the crew were all saved by the Midgetts. I was third officer on her at the time & going through my papers brought back old times. I was wondering if any of those brave men are alive today. If so I should like to hear from them. I do not know if you will receive this letter but I am taking a chance as I do not know the full address.
> I remain yours sincerely,
> VA Wild (ex-Master Mariner)

Wild addressed the envelop to simply, "Midgetts, Rodanthe, North Carolina."

# THE LIFESAVERS' LEGACY

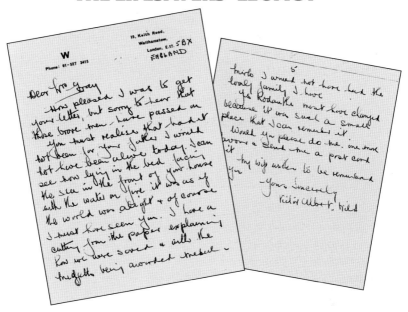

He posted it and hoped it might produce a reply. It did. The Rodanthe postmaster in 1970 had no idea to which of the many Midgetts to forward the letter, but when they opened it and read the words, they knew just the person who should receive it: 61-year-old Bethany Midgett Gray, Captain Johnny's pretty young daughter.

Over the next few months, Wild and Gray corresponded. Wild's handwritten replies complete the *Mirlo* story. "How pleased I was to get your letter, but sorry to hear that those brave men have passed on," he wrote. "I have a cutting from the papers explaining how we were saved & with the Midgetts being awarded medals given by our late King George to the brave men. ... When our little one came we named her Mirlo after the name of the ship. ... My daughter Mirlo is now married with a son and daughter again named Mirlo."

When one reads Wild's letters to Bethany Gray, the lessons of history and the true essence of the lifesavers' legacy becomes evident. It is here where the ripples in the pond extend, emanating from that moment at 5 p.m. on the 16th of August 1918, when motor surfboat No. 1046 gained the open ocean and proceeded to rescue the 42 men of the steam tanker *Mirlo*. The legacy of Chicamacomico's lifesavers today can be found not just in medals or silver cups or Coast Guard cutters or the preservation of a historic place—it is found in the flesh and blood and lives of families who would not have lived had it not been for John Allen Midgett's unselfish act of courage 100 years ago.

"You must realize that had it not been for your father that I would not have been alive today," Wild wrote from London to Bethany a few months before he died in December 1970. "I can see now lying in the bed facing the sea in the front of your house with the water on fire. It was if the world was alight & of course I must have seen you. ... Will you convey to your family & brothers my regards and tell them that if it had not been for a brave man saving us off the oil tanker *Mirlo* I would not have had the lovely family I have."

CHA photo.

# THE SEVENTH HERO

An all-important member of the 1918 Chicamacomico life-saving team survives to this day—the Beebe-McLellan self-bailing motor surfboat No. 1046—the seventh hero of the *Mirlo* rescue. The men involved in the *Mirlo* disaster are sadly all gone, but this remarkable participant in one of the greatest U.S. Coast Guard rescues in history lives on, the solitary tangible link to the 1918 story.

The slender chain of sandy barrier islands known as North Carolina's Outer Banks have been the scene of hundreds of years of notable events in U.S. history, arguably a greater number of historical events per square mile than anywhere in America. Little evidence of that history has remained. Some artifacts like the Wright brothers' 1903 flyer at Washington, D.C.'s Smithsonian are displayed far beyond the physical context in which they made history. But that is not the case with Coast Guard surfboat No. 1046.

Perfectly preserved at Rodanthe's U.S. Life-Saving Station Chicamacomico Historic Site, the venerable surfboat sits in her boathouse as if she is ready and waiting for her Coast Guard lifesavers to take her to sea on another rescue. Like her former keeper, Captain Johnny, the surfboat possesses a gentle, humble, kindly countenance that belies her incredible strength, seaworthiness, and indomitable spirit. Surfboat No. 1046 is an American treasure, an icon representing the honorable tradition of life-saving and some of the greatest heroes of American maritime history. The historic site where this extraordinary surfboat can be seen is an excellent place to visit and connect with the past and relive the thrilling moments of the 1918 *Mirlo* rescue. You can stand in the watch tower and scan the ocean horizon through the same windows as did Leroy Midgett. You can tour the station's rooms where the *Mirlo* survivors slept for the night. And you can stand beside the 25-foot-long surfboat No. 1046 and pretend to be one of the six brave men who launched her into the burning sea.

# NOTES

1. Operations Orders, "o-Befehl für U-*117*, 21 June 1918, Bundes-und Militärarchiv: RM 5/6428, 59-57. Found in *Tin Pots and Pirate Ships*, 273.
2. Ibid.
3. Beesly, Patrick. *Room 40: British Naval Intelligence*, 1914–1918. (London: Hamish Hamilton, 1982). 69-70.
4. The mission objective from the German perspective was the same as expressed by Germany's Commander-in-Chief U-boats, Vice-Admiral Ernst Ritter von Mann who stated that the purpose was to "draw off to America escort forces active in British waters." *Tin Pots and Pirate Ships*, p. 228.
5. HMT *Olympic*'s younger sister-ships RMS *Titanic* and HMHS *Britannic* had been sunk by an iceberg and a German mine respectively.
6. *Tin Pots*, 277.
7. Biography of John Allen Midgett, Jr. by Nell Wise Wechter, *Dictionary of North Carolina Biography*, edited by William S. Powell. Chapel Hill: University of North Carolina Press, 1979-1996.
8. War Diary, U-*151*, found in *Tin Pots and Pirate Ships*, 244
9. The first historic British ship-based air-raid on the German naval forces at Cuxhaven was conducted on December 25, 1914.
10. Third officer V.A. Wild account.
11. Some previously published accounts of the *Mirlo* story have stated that the tanker was going to make a stop at Norfolk before continuing on to New York but this notion is not supported by statements by Third officer V.A. Wild who wrote that after reaching the Wimble Shoals buoy, the tanker was to alter its course directly for the entrance to New York's Ambrose Channel.
12. "The Paravane and Its Inventor," *Munsey's Magazine*, Volume 68, 1919, 542-543.
13. The times for this narrative have been adapted to the local (Hatteras Island) eastern daylight time. The corresponding times indicated in the *Mirlo* records, including Capt. Williams's statement, show that the ship's clocks were set one hour earlier than those at Chicamacomico Coast Guard Station.
14. *Regulations of the Life-Saving Service of 1899*, Article VI "Action at Wrecks," Section 252, page 58.
15. James, Henry J.,*German Subs in Yankee Waters: First World War*, New York, Gotham House [c1940]
16. Wild's estimation of the times have been adjusted to conform to Chicamacomico Coast Guard Station time.
17. Benzol and benzene are known carcinogens. Significant exposure to benzol fumes may have caused aplastic anemia, leukemia, and multiple myeloma. Benzol was a notorious cause of bone marrow failure. In 1948 the American Petroleum Institute stated that "the only absolutely safe concentration for benzene (benzol) is zero. There is no safe exposure level; even tiny amounts can cause harm." It is not known if any of the survivors of the *Mirlo* disaster or members of the Chicamacomico crew later suffered from the carcinogenic effects of benzol exposure.
18, "Sea Stories Abound Within Chicamacomico's Old Walls," Paul Philips, writer, NC Travel & Tourism Division. *The Robesonian*, Dec. 16, 1977.
19. The 168-foot-long SS *Legonia II* was formerly the private yacht of Baltimore businessman and Johns Hopkins Hospital benefactor William B. Hurst. Some accounts of the *Mirlo* story have confused Hurst with publisher William R. Hearst.
20. *Alexandria Gazette,* 24 May 1919.
21. Officially, the medal was known as a Gold Foreign Service Medal.
22. "Our Eastern Shoals: A Foreign Land," William A. Blair. T*he High Point Enterprise*, Aug. 14,1938, 3.

# SELECT BIBLIOGRAPHY

## Primary Sources

Chicamacomico U.S. Coast Guard Station logs
U-boat log of U-*117* translations by Edwin Bearss and Michael Lowery
Victor Albert Wild letters, NPS Cape Hatteras National Seashore
Statement of Capt. W. R. Williams, SS *Mirlo*
Statement of Chief Boatswain John Allen Midgett
Resource Studies Project—Chicamacomico, Part Six, Oct. 1965, Edwin C. Bearss, NPS Research Historian

## Secondary Sources

Annual Report of the United States Coast Guard 1920.

Beesly, Patrick, *Room 40: British Naval Intelligence, 1914–1918.* (London: Hamish Hamilton, 1982).

Clark, William Bell, *When U-boats Came to America*, (Boston: Little, Brown, and Company, 1929).

*German Submarine Activities on the Atlantic Coast of the United States and Canada*, Office of Naval Records and Library, (Washington: Govt. Print. Office, 1920).

Hadley, Michael L., Sarty, Roger, *Tin-Pots and Pirate Ships: Canadian Naval Forces and German Sea Raiders 1880-1918* (Quebec: McGill-Queen's University Press, 1991).

James, Henry J., *German Subs in Yankee Waters: First World War*, (New York: Gotham House, 1940).

Noble, Dennis L., *Rescued by the U.S. Coast Guard: Great Acts of Heroism Since 1878.* (Annapolis, MD: Naval Institute Press, 2005).

Shanks, Ralph; York, Wick, *The U.S. Life-Saving Service—Heroes, Rescues and Architecture of the Early Coast Guard.* (Petaluma: Costaño Books, 1996).

Sims, RADM William Snowden, *The Victory at Sea*, (London: J. Murray, 1920).

The Official U.S. Bulletin, September 5, 1918.

United States Naval Institute *Proceedings*, July 1919, Vol. 45, No. 197.

Wechter, Nell Wise, *The Mighty Midgetts of Chicamacomico*, (Manteo, N.C.: Times Printing Company, Inc. 1974).

Kevin P. Duffus photo.

# ACKNOWLEDGEMENTS

I wish to extend my most-heartfelt appreciation to the Chicamacomico Historical Association for its support and research assistance that made this book possible, in particular board members John Griffin and Ralph Buxton, and Chicamacomico Historic Site and Museum Manager Dinah Beveridge. This project would not have succeeded without the support of Don and Catharine Bryan. Gee Gee Rosell of Buxton Village Books deserves extra credit for her persistent encouragement and enthusiasm. I am also grateful to my editor Vicky Jarrett. Artist Austin Dwyer perfectly captured the drama of the *Mirlo* rescue in his two exceptional paintings. People who helped with the research include Jami Lanier, Juanita Wescott, Warren Wrenn, Tama Creef, Sara Whitford, and Stuart Parks. I thank Peter Schulz of Deutsches U-Boot Museum Cuxhaven for his help in providing the rare *U-117* photos. My efforts were greatly aided by the earlier work of Ed Bearss, Michael Lowery, and the Midgett family. I am also honored to have as friends, Joseph Schwarzer, Bill Leslie, Bland Simpson, and Stanley So. Without the correspondence and eyewitness testimony of Victor Albert Wild, this story would have been incomplete—I have spent many hours trying to locate Wild's granddaughter, Mirlo, unsuccessfully but I will keep trying. Lastly, as she has done for each of my six books, my wife Susan has offered brilliant suggestions, helped to proofread, and has patiently filled-in for me—even mowing the grass!—while I have had to neglect my many obligations and chores.

Kevin Duffus
June 1, 2018

# CHICAMACOMICO
## Life-Saving Station Historic Site and Museum

*"The best preserved and most authentic of all life-saving stations."*
Richard L. Chenery, *Old Coast Guard Stations*

Chicamacomico Life-Saving Station Historic Site and Museum is the only museum of its kind existing in North Carolina. It stands as a place to re-visit the wrecks, rescues, and daily events that the men of the U.S. Life-Saving Service experienced on the Outer Banks. It is one of the most complete Life-Saving Station sites remaining in the United States and the only one designated as a teaching museum.

This unique site encompasses seven acres and contains eight original buildings: the 1874 station and its cookhouse and water tank, the 1911 station and its four outbuildings, cistern and two water tanks, and a 1907 home that is filled with artifacts and period pieces depicting early 20th century life on Hatteras Island.

The Chicamacomico Historical Association is a private, nonprofit organization whose sole purpose is to restore, preserve, protect, and interpret the buildings, grounds, and history of Chicamacomico Life-Saving Station and the early Coast Guard on the Outer Banks. Building restoration, exhibit development, and historical research are funded by donors and private grants, and augmented by other limited funding. No regular state or federal funding is received. Memberships are an important factor in our fundraising, and all contributions are tax deductible.

Visit www.chicamacomico.org
or call for hours of operation and fees.

**Call: 252-987-1552**
**Location: NC Hwy. 12—MP 39.5—Rodanthe, NC**

## About the Author

Kevin P. Duffus is an award-winning filmmaker, researcher, and investigative journalist of historical events. In 2002, he solved the *140-year-old Civil War mystery of the lost Cape Hatteras Lighthouse Fresnel lens.*

He is the author of *War Zone—World War II Off the North Carolina Coast; The Lost Light—A Civil War Mystery; The Last Days of Black Beard the Pirate; Shipwrecks of the Outer Banks—An Illustrated Guide;* and *The Story of Cape Fear and Bald Head Island.* He was named the 2014 Historian of the Year by the NC Society of Historians.

Kevin Duffus is available to speak to groups of 50 people or more. Send E-mail requests to: looking_glass@earthlink.net.

### Books

$40.00

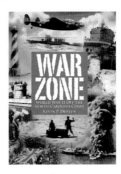
$24.95

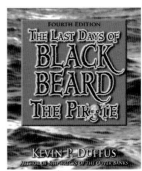
$24.95

$24.95

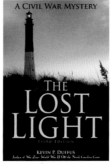
$20.00

$14.95

### DVDs

$19.95

$19.95

$19.95

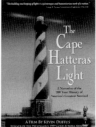
$19.95

Looking Glass Productions, Inc.
P.O. Box 561
Waynesville, NC  28786

1-828-648-2148

www.kevinduffus.com
www.thelostlight.com